Living & Working
in Greece

Living & Working in Greece

*Your guide to a successful
short or long-term stay*

PETER REYNOLDS
2nd edition

How To Books

DEDICATION

This book is dedicated to my loving wife
Chrissie, without whose constant support in
helping me fulfil a long cherished pipe-dream,
none of this would have been possible.

Published by How To Books Ltd,
3 Newtec Place, Magdalen Road,
Oxford OX4 1RE, United Kingdom.
Tel: (01865) 793806. Fax: (01865) 248780.

First edition 1996
Second edition 2001

British Library Cataloguing in Publication Data
A catalogue record for this book is available from
the British Library.

Cartoons by Mike Flanagan
Cover design by Shireen Nathoo Design
Cover image PhotoDisc

Produced for How To Books by Deer Park Productions
Typeset by Anneset, Weston-super-Mare, North Somerset
Printed and bound by Cromwell Press, Trowbridge, Wiltshire

NOTE: The material contained in this book is set out in good faith for
general guidance and no liability can be accepted for loss or expense
incurred as a result of relying in particular circumstances on statements
made in the book. Laws and regulations are complex and liable to
change, and readers should check the current position with the relevant
authorities before making personal arrangements.

Contents

List of Illustrations

Preface

Back in the early 1990's when we first seriously considered the idea of buying a property in Greece, we were surprised at the lack of material on living and working in Greece, let alone an authoritative tome on purchasing property. As a result, and fuelled by many years' experience of the Greek way of life, I decided with the kind backing and support of my publisher, to address the opportunity. This book is dedicated to all lovers of Greece who have fallen hopelessly for its charms.

Greece is a frustrating yet immensely beautiful country, as you will soon discover if you are contemplating a move there. Western culture, so evident in Athens and in a few of the larger cities, contrasts starkly with the simplistic and relaxed Eastern approach to life in the country and on the islands. Greece is truly the convergence of two cultures, where East meets West.

Bear in mind, however, Greece is not for the well organised, meticulous and tidy person. Friendship, *filoxenía* (hospitality), conversation and an overall sense of wellbeing matter far more to the Greeks than efficiency and systems, which is all well and good until you want to get something done! Be prepared for the Greek approach of *ávrio* (tomorrow) when it comes to anything remotely involving paperwork.

I have tried to show the true Greece without viewing life through rose-tinted spectacles. The observations and comments I make are based on my own impressions and should be viewed only as a guide to what you may expect, but hopefully, the result is a practical and usable everyday handbook to be dipped into for information ranging from health and welfare issues right through to the practicalities of identifying and opening the right bank account. Whether you are a student, professional, a retired person, or simply an interested traveller, you should find many of your initial questions answered, and advice on where to seek answers to more complicated matters.

Finally, I would like to thank the many people and organisations who have helped me over the months with the book's contents. If this book helps to illustrate the warmth and friendship of the wonderful Greek people and their most beautiful country, then I will be content. *Kaló Taxídhi.*

The research into the second edition of this handbook was mostly carried out in Athens during May 2000. On reviewing the changes to the first edition printed some four years before, I was staggered to find that over 300 corrections were necessary. In that time Greece has moved from a position of galloping inflation, poor GDP per capita and certain 'Eastern' approaches to health, welfare, commerce and education to an enlightened, pro-European country eagerly awaiting acceptance as the thirteenth member state of the EMU, relishing the prospect of hosting the Olympic Games in 2004, and investing heavily in a new transportation and telecommunications programme.

Yet, in many other respects, little has changed. The kaleidoscope of differing cultures remains very much in evidence. The larger cities are globalising, everywhere now there is McDonalds, Wendy's, Goodies *etc* and the proliferation of mobile phones has been immense, but wander out into the country, up to the mountain villages and for many life has been unaltered by the pace of technological change. The evening *volta* (the slow, evening perambulations down the streets in best clothes) continues as it has over the centuries, the *panagíria* (party) to celebrate a namesake day still remains the focus of village life.

In another five years' time technology will undoubtedly have continued unabated to transform the face of the larger cities – the Internet still remains very much in its infancy at the moment. But for many the simple pleasures of *filoxenía*, friendship and camaraderie, will continue to satiate the traveller's dream, as portrayed by John Fowles in *The Magus*: 'It was like a journey into space. I was standing on Mars, knee-deep in thyme, under a sky that seemed never to have known dust or cloud.'

Peter Reynolds

1

Introducing Greece

Yá Sas (hello) and *Hérete* (welcome) to Greece, situated at the cross-roads of three continents in the southern part of the Balkan peninsula in the Eastern Mediterranean, a beautiful country, when you get to know it, encapsulated in this quotation from the novelist Henry Miller, 'In one way or another, at some time or other, we have all been there, even if only in a dream.'

CONSIDERING ITS LOCATION

Greece has a total area in excess of 130,000 square kilometres and consists of mainland and islands which occupy approximately 20 per cent of the total area and contribute to Greece's severely indented coastline of over 15,000 kilometres. Greece borders on the north with Albania, the former Yugoslav Republic of Macedonia, Bulgaria and on the north east with Turkey. It is Europe's closest link to the Middle East. With the European Union operating as a single market, Greece is ideally situated as an entry port to the EU from the Middle East, North Africa and most of the north-east Balkan countries. Greece is surrounded on three sides by sea: the Aegean in the east, the Ionian in the west and the sea of Crete in the south.

EXPLORING THE COUNTRY

Over 80 per cent of Greece's land space is covered by mountains, the highest of which is Mount Olympus at 2,917 metres in the east central region. The principal mountain range, Pindus, runs north to south in western Greece. Less than 30 per cent of the total land is cultivated. Expansive plains abound in Thessaly and Macedonia and to a lesser extent in north west Peloponnese, a peninsula which was connected to the rest of the mainland by the Isthmus of Corinth. The Corinth Canal, completed in 1893, makes an artificial island of the Peloponnese.

Fig. 1. Map of Greece.

Visiting islands

There are more than 1,400 islands in Greece, but only 166 of them are recognised as 'inhabited', although only about 55 of these have permanent communities of any real significance. The islands account for less than 20 per cent of the total area of the country. The largest is Crete followed in size by Évvia. Other well known islands include:

- Aegean
    — Lésvos
    — Sámos
    — Thássos

- Argo-Saronic
    — Aegina
    — Póros
    — Spétses

- Cyclades
  — Míkonos
  — Náxos
  — Páros

- Dodecanese
  — Kálimnos
  — Kos
  — Rhodes

- Ionian
  — Corfu
  — Kefaloniá
  — Zákinthos

- Sporades
  — Alónissos
  — Skíathos
  — Skópelos

Pros and cons of life on the islands

Pros

- Stunning scenery — you are never far from the beach and sea.

- Seclusion — a real chance to get away from it all, especially outside the towns and main villages.

- Quality of life — a slower, more relaxed pace. Nothing is too much trouble.

Cons

- Communication — ferries will not run as frequently in the winter or in bad weather, or when they are on strike. You could be cut off from the mainland for weeks or months at a time.

- Transport — not necessarily always available, or when it is, it may not be regular or reliable depending on the size of the island.

- Water — fresh water is bound to be limited, and especially in the summer you run the real risk of having it severely rationed.

Enjoying the climate

The Greek islands are renowned for a balmy Mediterranean climate, with short mild winters and long, hot, dry summers. The mountain areas are much cooler, with considerable rain in the summer months. Frost and snow are rare on the mainland, but the mountains are covered with snow in the winter. Greece boasts 360 sunny days a year.

Looking at the people

Greece has the distinction of being the most unpopulated country in Europe, containing just about ten and a half million inhabitants and growing slowly, with a density of approximately 80 people per square kilometre. The available labour force is about four-and-a-half million, but almost ten per cent of this working population is unemployed. Around half of the inhabitants live in the Attica area, which is largely Athens and Piraeus, where also more than half of the Greek industry is located. Thessaloniki in northern Greece houses approximately one million and Pátras in the west Peloponnese, Heraklion on the island of Crete and mainland Volos are the other major cities with a population of over 100,000.

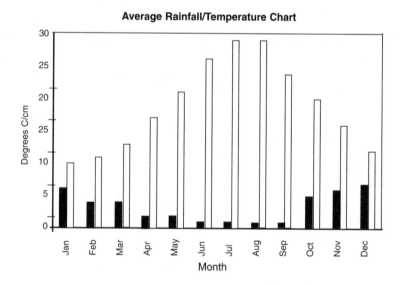

Fig. 2. Average rainfall/temperature chart.

Greeks living abroad

In addition to the domestic population, it is estimated that there is a diaspora of about 11–12 million Greeks living abroad, although no official figure is recorded. The main countries are USA, Australia, the Soviet Republic and Cyprus.

In addition to the main centres, there are estimated to be about 5,000 Greeks together with around 8,000 students living in the UK.

HOW IS GREECE GOVERNED?

Greek civilisation dates back to ancient times, and is reputedly the birthplace of democracy. Despite the fact that at various times Greece had been under foreign rule, it has, since the 19th century, emerged as an independent nation, and despite the many years of foreign occupation has managed to maintain its traditions, roots and its own language.

Greece is a Presidential Parliamentary Democracy. The head of state is the President, who is elected for a five year period by the Parliament. The functions of the state are separated into three divisions: legislative, executive and judicial.

Examining legislative affairs

The legislative authority is vested in Parliament and the President. Parliament comprises 300 members elected by popular vote for a four year term. Laws are voted on by Parliament and ratified by the President in order to be enacted.

After a political career spanning some 60 years, the veteran President Karamanlis handed in his resignation to Parliament in March 1995, two months ahead of the end of his elected five year term of office, clearing the way for the President-elect, Costis Stephanopoulos. Respected across the political spectrum, Mr Stephanopoulos, 20 years the junior of Mr Karamanlis, has turned out to be more outspoken on foreign and domestic issues than his predecessors in the largely ceremonial post.

Considering the executive

The executive division, the Government, is headed by the Prime Minister, who is normally the leader of the political party with the majority of Parliamentary seats, and the cabinet members who function as heads of the various ministries. A national referendum held on 8 December 1974 abolished the monarchy and established a republic, following the seven year 'Junta' or military dictatorship.

Greece has had three major political parties since 1974. The centre-right

Nea Demokráti (New Democracy) party ruled between November 1974 and October 1981 and returned to power in April 1990. The centre-left *PASOK* (Panhellenic Socialist Movement) party ruled between October 1981 and June 1989. The *KKE* (Communist) party is also significant. During a brief period between June 1989 and April 1990, the country was ruled by coalition governments as elections in both June and November 1989 failed to provide any party with an absolute majority in Parliament.

The present Prime Minister Costas Simitis is the leader of *PASOK,* the Socialist party that was re-elected following the 1996 elections. His second period in office was ratified at the General Elections held on 10 April 2000. In a keenly contested battle the Socialists took 158 seats in Parliament, therefore returning just less than 44 per cent of the vote. *Nea Demokráti* polled slightly less than 43 per cent.

Studying judicial matters

The judicial division is independent of Parliament and government and is divided into civil, criminal and administrative sections. For administration purposes Greece is divided into a number of *nomi* (districts) which are governed by *nomarches* (local administrations) appointed by the government.

Greece is a member of a number of international bodies including the Council of Europe, the United Nations, the North Atlantic Treaty Organisation (NATO), the Organisation of Economic Co-Operation and Development (OECD) and the International Monetary Fund (IMF).

Since 1981 Greece has been a full member of the European Union (EU) after being an associate member since 1962. The Treaty of Accession provided for transitional periods of various lengths so that the local legislation could be smoothly integrated with that of the EU in areas such as the movement of labour, customs duties and exchange controls. Greece has a European bias and was one of the first EU member states to ratify the Maastricht Treaty through the almost unanimous vote of the Greek Parliament.

Over the last five years the Greek economy has taken tremendous strides forward and, as a result, Greece finally joined the European Monetary Union (EMU) on 1 January 2001 following ratification at the European summit held in Portugal on 16 June 2000. The drachma was admitted to the Exchange Rate Mechanisms on 14 March 1998. Inflation currently stands at two-and-three-quarter per cent (having fallen from over 25 per cent in the 1980s) whilst interest rates are falling and general public debt is declining. GDP has now grown for the third consecutive year and represents three-and-a-half per cent. Overall

confidence in business circles has been at an all time high as represent-
ed by stock valuations on the Athens Bourse (stock market).

WHAT MAKES GREECE TICK?

Agriculture plays an important role in the Greek economy. Small industrial concerns established in the period after World War I were, to a large
extent, destroyed during World War II and the subsequent civil war.
Development of the manufacturing sector of the economy since then has
been hampered by the lack of fuel and difficulties in utilising the hydro-
electric potential of the country. By 1970, however, the contribution of
manufacturing to the annual national output surpassed that of agriculture
for the first time. Two main sources of income for Greece are shipping
and tourism. The production of petroleum from fields in the northern
Aegean Sea began to aid the economy in the early 1980s. Greece also
receives considerable 'invisible income' in the form of EU grants and
subsidies.

Trading with the UK

Always a significant trading partner, the UK's share of Greek imports,
which traditionally has been minimal, began to increase in 1987 and is
now a little over five per cent. The UK is the fifth largest exporter to
Greece behind Germany, Italy, France and the Netherlands.

British exports to Greece are increasing steadily, currently amounting
to over nine hundred million pounds. This makes the Greek market one
of the faster-growing, although still the smallest UK export market in the
European Union. By contrast, imports from Greece at currently less than
three hundred million pounds are gradually declining.

Farming and harvesting

About 25 per cent of the Greek workforce is engaged in farming.
Agriculture accounts for about 15 per cent of the gross domestic product (GDP), but productivity does not match the investment made in the
agricultural sector of the economy. Farms are small as inheritance over
the years has sub-divided once sizeable plots. Yields are low due to the
dryness and erosion of the soil, and consequently it is difficult to use
mechanised equipment efficiently. It is becoming increasingly notice-
able that much of Greece's agricultural land (especially near to towns) is
being given over to industrial and domestic development.

The Greek government owns about two thirds of the forestland and has taken steps to replace the trees that were destroyed during World War II. Income from the fishing industry is minimal whilst sponges are the leading marine commodity produced for export.

Mining for minerals
Although mining is of relatively little importance to the Greek economy, a considerable variety of mineral deposits is exploited and exported including lignite, bauxite, iron ore and magnesite. Marble continues to be quarried and exported in large quantities.

Summarising manufacturing
About 20 per cent of the workforce is engaged in manufacturing producing:

- basic metal products
- cement
- chemicals
- clothing and textiles
- food and drink
- tobacco
- wine and beer.

About 90 per cent of Greece's electricity is produced in thermal facilities burning lignite, coal or refined petroleum, and the rest is generated in hydro-electric installations, which are mainly situated on the Akeloos River in the Pindus mountains.

Looking at major projects
Greece has embarked on a major infrastructure development programme that will enable the country to become South Europe's hub for air, road and ship transport both to and from eastern and western Europe.

There are substantial major public sector projects in Greece at various stages of development. Mostly funded with EU grant aid, (18.5 billion ECU for the five-year period 1994–1999, a further 26.6 billion ECU has been earmarked for 2000–2006) the major projects include:

- Athens and Thessaloniki underground systems
- Athens' second international airport at Spata
- additional airport projects including Thessaloniki, Rhodes and Corfu

- modernisation of the railway system including Athens–Thessalonikí–Idomeni line
- mobile telecommunications
- natural gas implementation in Athens, Thessaloniki, Laríssa and Volos
- power generation plants
- new ports at Rhodes, Mikonós, Corfu, Mytilini and Souda
- tramways including Athens and Kalamata
- tunnels and bridges including Rion–Antirron, Akfion–Preveza connection
- various motorways and new roads including modernising the road system of Attica basin
- water and sewage.

EXPLORING THE GLORIOUS PAST

Prima facie evidence would suggest that the recorded history of Greece covers a period in excess of 3,000 years. Many early relics of Greek civilisation are to be found in the various museums in Athens and Thessaloniki, although there have been a number of findings going back some 5,000 years to the Iron and Stone Ages.

Introducing the Geometric and Archaic period

This period from the 11th to the 8th century BC is known as the 'Geometric period' because of the geometric designs which were dominant in Greek art at the time. The Geometric period was followed by the 'Archaic era', which covers the 8th to the 5th century BC. This era was of great importance to the ancient Greek cities, particularly Athens and Sparta, which pioneered developments in the years immediately following.

Moving into a Classical era

The 5th and 4th centuries BC are regarded as the 'Classical years' during which the ancient Greek civilisation was at its mightiest. After a series of successful battles, the Persian attempts to conquer Greece in the years 490–479 BC were finally thwarted and the Greek cities enjoyed a period of peace and tranquillity during which the arts flourished. This was the period when the theatrical tragedies of poets Aeschylus, Sophocles and Euripides provided the foundation for classical drama, whilst the writings of Aristophanes introduced satirical comedy. The letters of Socrates and his pupil Plato illustrate the great debates of knowledge and meaning. During this time the monuments of the Acropolis in Athens were built, of which the most important is the Parthenon, a temple dedicated to Goddess Athena whose construction lasted from 447–432 BC. The Parthenon, gradually fading away and now closed to the public, remains the premier landmark in Athens today. It has been roped off from the public since 1983 when the Parthenon Restoration project commenced, funded by the Greek Government and EU funds.

The Peloponnesian War between Athens and Sparta (431–404 BC) resulted in the loss of power in towns and states of southern Greece. This gave birth to the ascendancy of Thebes and defeat of Sparta in the northern state of Macedonia, whose King Philip managed to unite all Greeks. Macedonia became the lynchpin in Greek affairs during the 4th century BC. Philip was succeeded by his son Alexander the Great, who set about defeating the Persians and effectively progressing the influence of Greece throughout the Middle East.

Progressing through Hellenistic years

After the death of Alexander the Great in 323 BC, the 'Hellenistic years' were born during which the Greek civilisation went through a revitalisation not only in Greece, but also throughout the Middle East where Greek monarchies were installed. However, on-going civil wars reduced the Greek powers further and the country was eventually overcome by the Romans in 146 BC.

Moving the seat of the Roman Empire

Constantine the Great transferred the seat of the Roman Empire in 330 AD to a new city named after him, Constantinople. In 395 AD the Roman Empire was divided between the west and the east with Constantinople as its capital. The eastern Roman Empire under the influence of the Greek civilisation was gradually hellenised and developed into the Byzantine Empire, retaining language and culture as its hallmarks. The Byzantine Empire came to an abrupt end in 1453 AD with the fall of Constantinople to the Ottoman Turks. Crete was the last bastion to fall to the Turks, surviving a further 400 years.

Stealing the marbles

Many relics and artifacts of the Byzantine era can now be seen at the British Museum in London, where you will also find the Parthenon sculptures or 'Elgin Marbles' removed from the Parthenon by the British diplomat Thomas Bruce, seventh Earl of Elgin, in 1806 and transported back to England, after acquiring the sculptures from the Turks to prevent them being crushed for building materials. At the time Lord Elgin was criticised for removing priceless national treasures. After a ten year struggle he persuaded the British government to buy the marbles and place them in the British Museum. The chief pieces by the 5th century BC master Phidias are from the frieze and tympani of the Parthenon. Until the death in 1995 of Melina Mercouri, the film star who became the Greek Minister for Culture, there appeared to be a chance, albeit a slim one, that one day the tablets would be returned to their rightful resting place.

Getting into hot water
In recent months the Marbles have become a leading issue in the international debate over restitution of cultural heritage. Fuelled about their care and cleaning, the Greek authorities are pressing relentlessly for the homecoming of *ta marmara*. One deadline mentioned is 2004 when the Olympic Games are scheduled to be held in Athens. The dispute now revolves around the unfortunate 'over-cleaning' with chisels and scrapers in 1937–38 arranged by the art dealer Lord Duveen. The somewhat over-zealous rubbing was carried out to fit in with the then notion of positive whiteness. However, as soon as the damage was discovered the work was stopped.

Studying the Wars of Independence
Greece remained under Ottoman rule for nearly 400 years until the outbreak of the Greek revolution in 1821 and the ensuing War of Independence which led to the creation of the modern Greek state in 1827.

The Greek War of Independence (1821-33) liberated the city of Athens from the Turks and made it the capital of modern Greece. Previously Náfplion on the Peloponnese with its wonderful Venetian fortress had held the honour of capital city. Athens was largely rebuilt during the reign of King Otto (1832-62) by German architects, notably Eduard Schaubert.

It took well over a century and successive Wars of Independence for the northern states of Greece to overcome foreign rule and rejoin the southern states as a united independent country.

WHAT ABOUT OTHER INFORMATION?

Moving on now from the background of Greece, some interesting general points are worthy of mention.

Putting up with the bureaucracy

This is the basis of life in Greece, so please maintain the status quo. Few Greek officials will actually make a positive decision — they will always refer your case to another colleague in another office, on another day. Also, it is not possible to write to a Greek Ministry concerning your business. You have to appear personally with a written application (*dethsh*), which is eventually presented to the *protokolo* normally with a 50 or 100 GRD stamp, and then await results. However, it is wise to pursue your case with personal visits to enhance the possibility of a favourable answer.

Finding out about religion

The Greek Orthodox Church is firmly established and dominates the architectural and religious presence. The Archbishop of Athens and all Greece heads the Church which is specially governed by a synod of the bishops and other leading members. Most of the Church's income comes from its huge investment in property going back over the years, although a certain amount arises from the state. As in many other western cultures, the Church is gradually losing its appeal particularly to the younger generation. The institution of civil marriage was forced on the Church by the government following wide-sweeping reforms in 1981. Before then, Greeks who married abroad by civil ceremony were not accepted as married under civil law, nor was marriage in another church accepted as valid by the Greek Orthodox.

The Church still owns a substantial stockpile of agricultural land which the government is trying to reclaim and put to constructive use for farming and co-operative projects. It is also interesting to note that priests are paid a salary by the government.

Watch out for time differences

Greece is two hours ahead of Greenwich Mean Time (GMT). From the last Sunday in March until the last Sunday in September, the clocks are advanced one hour to take advantage of the extra daylight.

Getting used to the money

The monetary unit of Greece is the *dhrahmí* (drachma). The most common notes are those of 100 (slowly being faded out), 500, 1,000, 5,000, 10,000 and 20,000. Theoretically, coins come in denominations of one, two, five, ten, 20, 50, 100 *dhrahmés*, although you would be hard pushed to find some of the smaller denomination coins. The *dhrahmí* was subdivided into one hundred *leptá* (unit) but these have now been withdrawn

Table of Greek National Holidays

2001

New Years Day (*Protochroniá*)	1 January
Epiphany Day (*ton Theofaníon*)	6 January
Ash or Clean Monday (*Katharí Deftéra*)	26 February*
Greek Independence Day (*Ikosti Pémti*)	25 March
Good Friday (*Megali Paraskeví*)	13 April*
Easter Sunday (*Aghion Páskha*)	15 April*
Easter Monday (*Deftéra ton Páscha*)	16 April*
May Day (*Protomagiá*)	1 May
Ascension Whit Monday (*Análipsis ton Agíou*)	4 June*
Assumption Day (*Dekapendávgoustos tis Panagías*)	15 August
No (Ochi) Day (*Ikosti Ogdói Oktovríou*)	28 October
Christmas Day (*Christoúgenna*)	25 December
Boxing or St Stephen's Day (*Défteri iméra ton Christougénnon*)	26 December

Fig. 3. Greek holidays 2001.

from circulation. Whilst in the UK, changing sterling into GRD is probably best done at the Post Office, as they only charge minimal commission. In Greece, changing money at the *tachidromío* (Post Office) used to
be the least expensive route at a fixed commission charge of 800 GRD
irrespective of value changed. However, there are now automated teller
machines (ATMs) in most of the larger cities where you can obtain local
currency at a competitive rate of exchange without incurring bank
charges.

At the time of writing, the value of the Greek drachma was aproxi-
mately 570 to the pound sterling. The drachma has devalued by about
one-third over the last two years. Good news if you're a tourist, not such
good news if you own a holiday home. However, a condition of Greece
entering the EMU is that the drachma must be stabilised at 340.75 to the
Euro. As part of the monetary policy adjustments Lucas Papademos,
Governor of the Bank of Greece, has announced the gradual reduction
of bank reserve requirement from 12 per cent to the Euro zone's 2 per
cent. Throughout the book drachma are referred to as GRD.

Reducing inflation
Greece has been experiencing runaway inflation over the last 30 years,
but the rate has now come down from over 25 per cent in the early 1980s
to closer to just under 3 per cent, thanks to controls put on wages, reducing public debt and cutting down on tax evasion. The target is closer to
$2\frac{1}{2}$ per cent before the anticipated accession to the EMU scheduled for
January 2001. The cost of living in Greece is relatively low compared
with that of northern European countries.

Noting the public holidays
The national holidays (*argíes*) for 2001/2002 are shown in Figure 3. You
can expect banks, shops, offices *etc* to be closed. Dates marked with an
asterisk alter every year.

Ochi or No day commemorates the Greek resistance against the
Italians in 1940 and represents the first defeat of an Axis power in World
War II. This led to the German invasion. In addition to the above, Athens
celebrates its own patron saint's day, on October 3 — St Dionysios the
Areopagite (*tou Agíou Dionistíou*).

CASE STUDIES

During the course of the book, we will be following the trials and tribu-
lations of three sets of travellers to Greece, recounting various mishaps

and adventures appropriate to the subject matter. In this chapter, it is sufficient to introduce our itinerant friends to you.

Introducing Graham

Graham is a fresh-faced student currently studying for his first degree at university. He aims to travel to Greece as cheaply as possible for the duration of his eight week summer vacation, travelling around and getting seasonal work where he can.

Teaching in Greece

Tony and Wendy are a young couple with one child, who have decided to give up their teaching jobs in the UK and take a camper van to Greece. They hope to find gainful employment in education and make a go of raising their child overseas.

Retiring on Skíathos

John and Betty are a retired couple who have been holidaying in Greece for several years. They have bought a small stone cottage on the green and lush island of Skíathos and propose to spend part of the year in Greece renovating their property.

POINTS TO CONSIDER

1. Greece has a very traditional way of life. In certain areas, the more ebullient style of western life is frowned upon. Have you thought about how you will fit into this culture shock? How convinced are you that you can adapt?

2. With so many islands, mountainous areas, vast plains and mile upon mile of coastal beaches you should work out which area of Greece will best suit you. Communications, proximity of employment, available resources and climate should all be taken into account.

3. How worried are you that the political situation could change given possible border conflicts? Does the constant devaluation of the drachma make you nervous? How sure are you that you want a radically different life style?

2

Preparing to Travel

ASSESSING YOUR MOTIVES

Before you start getting yourself organised, you should ask yourself these simple questions:

- How keen am I to live in a hot climate?

- How happy am I to work Greek hours, with an early start, late lunch and very late dinner?

- Am I sufficiently extrovert to cope with the very outgoing Greeks?

- How much Greek am I prepared to learn? The more you can learn, the better.

- Can I accept the many idiosyncrasies of the Greek system which will drive me insane at times?

If you are happy that you can take all the above points in your stride, then stage one of your travel preparations is to sit down and consider the necessary procedures.

GETTING THE PAPERWORK STRAIGHT

This chapter provides background information on the paperwork and formalities that you will need to understand before leaving these shores.

Entering Greece

British citizens are permitted to enter Greece and to remain for three months from the date of entry without a visa or any other formality except customs examination. If this three month period is exceeded

without the permission of the Greek authorities, you may experience difficulties when trying to leave the country and in extreme cases prosecu-
tion for contravening the regulations may follow. However, an EU passport is not stamped on entry and is rarely, if ever, queried on departure.

Staying for a short while

British passport holders may live and work in Greece without any
restrictions, although if you wish to stay officially for longer than three
months, you should apply for a temporary residence permit to the Aliens
Bureau (*Ipiresía Allodhapón*). These are to be found in the larger cities.
Allow a full day for this as you will get pushed from pillar to post by the
Greek bureaucracy. In smaller towns and villages you can visit the local
police station. Addresses for the Aliens Bureau in Athens and its suburbs can be found in the Useful Addresses section.

Residence and work permits, valid for one year, may be renewed
annually for a period of up to five years. Upon expiry of the five year
period an application for an extension must be made.

Staying for a longer period

If you are planning to settle in Greece, you should obtain a Change of
Residence certificate which is issued by the Greek consular authorities
in London. This certificate lists only items which are subject to special
consumption tax in Greece. However, in reality people seldom obtain
such a certificate. Relevant addresses can be found in Useful Addresses.

Informing people

You should tell your relations and friends where you propose to live in
case you are needed in an emergency. In particular don't forget to inform
the Inland Revenue, Department of Health and Social Security, your
bank, solicitors and accountant. If you are staying in Greece for over
three months, you should register at the British embassy or nearest
British consulate as soon as possible and on 1 January of every year. You
should keep the authorities informed of any change of address and notify them when you leave Greece permanently.

Finding out about income tax

Income tax is payable by all persons who have an income arising in
Greece, subject to the amount of earnings, regardless of nationality or
place of residence. There is double taxation relief between the United
Kingdom and Greece to prevent a resident or non-resident being taxed
in both countries on the same income. Your local Inland Revenue office

should be able to advise you on this intricate matter. The address for the Greek Ministry of Finance can be found in Useful Addresses.

Transferring sickness benefit

If you are in receipt of sickness benefit in the UK, you may be able to transfer payment to Greece. Ask at your local Department of Social Security office in the UK for further information.

Transferring unemployment benefit

If you are entitled to UK unemployment benefit and have been claiming this benefit for at least four weeks, you may continue to receive it for up to three months whilst you seek work in Greece.

You should inform the office where you are claiming unemployment benefit of your intention to look for work elsewhere in the EU well in advance of your departure. Ask for form UBL22. If you satisfy the conditions of transfer of benefit overseas, your local office will advise the overseas branch, who will send you a form which you should take to the nearest Manpower Employment Organisation *Organisimos Apasholisseos Ergatikou Dynamikou* (OAED) office as soon as possible after you arrive in Greece.

PLANNING AHEAD

When considering a move to Greece, you cannot protect your health too highly. As Greek hospitals are fairly primitive by our standards, and nursing care is thin on the ground, you are strongly advised to take out the best form of medical insurance you can afford before leaving the UK.

Buying medical insurance

British passport holders are officially entitled to free medical care in Greece, provided they are permanently resident in the UK, on presentation of an E111 form, obtained by filling in form CM1 at a Department of Social Security office, Post Office or travel agent, at least a month before departure. Free, however, means admittance only to the lowest grade of state hospital, *yenikó nosokomío*, and does not include nursing care or the cost of medications. In practice, hospital staff tend to greet E111s with disdainful looks, and you might have to request reimbursement by the NHS upon your return home.

If you need prolonged medical care, it is far better to make use of private treatment, which is, as everywhere, expensive. For medical claims, keep receipts, including those from pharmacies (*farmakío*). You will have to pay for all private medical care on the spot (insurance claims can be processed if you have hospital treatment) but it can all be eventually claimed back.

Before leaving, obtain a copy of 'Health Advice for Travellers' (form T6) from any main Post Office.

Checking the small print
Whichever insurance company you choose, make sure that the cover for medical expenses is more than adequate. It helps, too, if there is an emergency 24 hour contact to take care of arrangements, including repatriation if necessary. Injuries caused while taking part in certain hazardous pursuits are normally excluded from medical cover. Look carefully at the policy, especially clauses and exemptions relating to riding mopeds and motorbikes.

Thinking about your medication
Most basic medical requirements — plasters, bandages, headache pills — can be bought in chemist shops (*farmakío*) in Greece. More than that, many drugs normally available in Britain only on prescription can be bought over the counter on demand and at reasonable prices. Note that codeine and drugs containing codeine are strictly banned in Greece, so be sure to exclude these from your luggage. Although similar, dosages of Greek drugs vary and are usually much stronger.

Getting immunised
No vaccinations or inoculations are required to enter Greece.

Finding a penfriend
There is no organisation in Greece that undertakes to find penfriends, but schools will sometimes arrange friends from amongst their pupils. It may be worth writing to one or two of the colleges in Athens or placing a small advertisement in one of the English speaking newspapers. Details can be found in Useful Addresses.

Checking your plugs
Electric current in Greece conforms to continental European standard *ie* 220–240 volts AC out of a double (un-earthed) or triple (earthed) round-pin socket. Therefore, travellers from the UK will require the appropriate plug adaptor. Be careful as there are two types of round pin plug and socket, the older ones thicker than the more modern types.

BRINGING YOUR POSSESSIONS INTO GREECE

This is an area fraught with legislation, which is not always published and not always consistent and is therefore worthy of close scrutiny.

Getting moved

If you are moving your household belongings from Britain to Greece, you may well require the services of an international removal firm. You are well advised to use one that takes responsibility for all the paperwork involved, which includes writing a full inventory in both English and Greek. Most removal firms also take charge of the packing and unpacking. The cost of the removal depends on the volume of your belongings. A full container load could cost around £5,000.

You should write to the British Association of Removers (address in Useful Addresses) who will send you a list of their international members together with a leaflet of handy hints for packaging.

Pros and cons of moving your possessions yourself

Pros

● Control — you will always be aware of exactly where the contents are and therefore when they will arrive.

● Cost — driving through Europe with a hire van containing all your possessions can be considerably less expensive than a professional move.

● Peace of mind — as you are responsible for your own possessions, you know that you will take good care of them.

Cons

● Paperwork — probably not having done it before, there is a lot to think about to make sure you have the correct inventory, driving documents etc with you.

● Customs — the real threat of being stopped by an over-zealous official and made to unpack the van whilst it is searched and you are questioned.

- Breakdown — if your hired van breaks down which means you miss your ferry crossing, then the whole episode could turn out to be a very expensive nightmare.

Restrictions on electrical appliances

The restrictions on personal effects have now been lifted for EU citizens; however, in reality you may be faced with minor problems when it comes to items such as electrical appliances.

Check the free importation of electrical goods as a UK TV does not work in Greece, but may be adapted by a TV engineer. Also, foreign system TVs *etc* may be bought in the UK *eg* Tottenham Court Road in London.

Moving household belongings

If you are moving from Britain to Greece, you are free to move your household belongings and personal effects, provided that you have owned them for more than three months and that you paid tax on purchasing them. The only way of proving this is with a sales invoice, so before you leave, gather together as many invoices as possible for items you intend to take. If you plan to move your household belongings in stages, you will still be exempt from paying tax, provided they are moved within six months of the date you acquire residence in Greece. Exemption from taxes also applies to those moving household effects from Britain to a holiday home in Greece, provided you are the owner of the property or have been paying rent for at least 12 months.

Paying import taxes

You may have to pay import taxes on certain items. For further information contact any Customs and Excise office in the UK before you leave, or, if you are in Greece, the local customs authority (*telonía*). If you are proposing to transport your worldly possessions yourself, then an unmarked van or estate car is preferable. Make sure before you leave that you draw up a list of furniture *etc*, declaring that you are moving the items from one EU country to another, with approximate values and stating that you are the owner of the items and that they are not for resale. If you are lucky enough to have a Greek friend in Britain, get this schedule drawn up in Greek as well, and then if you should get stopped by a zealous Greek official you have a chance of avoiding the need to unpack the vehicle and discuss the import taxes that the official may feel are payable locally — in some cases very locally!

Bringing in a boat

You should obtain a Certificate of Registration if you are considering importing a boat to Greece. The Small Ships Register, operated by the DVLA (see Useful Addresses), covers boats/ships less than 24 metres in length. Records include name, owner's details, description of the vessel and details of make or class.

Importing funds

Unlimited foreign exchange may be imported into Greece. It is always worth getting the 'pink currency slips' at the point of entering Greece as you may well need to prove sometime in the future how your wealth has been accumulated. There is no limit to the foreign currency used abroad by holders of credit cards.

Understanding custom allowances

The VAT exemption that duty free shops were enjoying with regard to sales to travellers within the EU has been abolished. You do not have to pay any tax or duty on goods you have bought in other EU countries for your own use. Guidelines for 'own use' goods are:

● 800 cigarettes or 200 cigars or 1kg of tobacco

● ten litres of spirits, 20 litres of fortified wine, 90 litres of wine, 110 litres of beer.

Checking your allowance

For travellers arriving from outside the EU:

● 200 cigarettes or 50 cigars or 250 grams of tobacco

● one litre of alcohol over 22 per cent volume or two litres of alcohol under 22 per cent volume or two litres of table wine

● 500 grams of coffee or 200 grams of coffee extracts and essences, 100 grams of tea or 40 grams tea extracts and essences

● 60 cc perfume, 250 cc toilet water

● other goods up to the value of £145.

If you bring in something worth more than the limit of £145 you will have to pay charges on the full value, not just on the value above £145.

What should I take?

Most leading brands of foods, clothes and other products are freely available in Greece. There are even a McDonalds, British Home Stores and Marks & Spencer, in Athens! Clearly, you will need to consider the geography of where you are going, weather conditions for the time of year and your own personal preferences.

As with most hot countries, Greece tends to be informal. In Athens, Thessaloniki and the other larger cities lightweight business suits and city dresses will be much in evidence.

From May until late September, Athens is unbearably hot and stuffy. Pack light clothing that does not crush easily. Come the winter and life gets cold and wet, therefore a warm jacket is a must. In spring and autumn, whilst the days are sunny, the evenings can quickly turn cool. Light sweaters, pullovers and a showerproof jacket will come in handy. A folding umbrella is useful as showers can strike without warning and are short, sharp, but heavy affairs.

Thinking about items not readily available

The following checklist contains a few of the items I have found over the years are hard to come by in Greece, disproportionately expensive or absolutely imperative:

- A good pair of sunglasses!

- Breakfast cereal — generally speaking the Greeks only have a basic but yet expensive range available depending on location.

- Comfortable shoes. Greek roads are hot and dusty.

- Orange squash — the British products taste much better, contain less sugar and are much cheaper. Greek natural juices, on the other hand, cannot be beaten with many different flavours and quality.

- Tea/coffee — tea bags are hard to come by away from the larger towns and coffee is very expensive.

- Universal sink plug — many Greek sinks will infuriate you as no plug is provided.

- Two pin plugs already attached to your electrical appliance.

- Mosquito nets/electric mosquito repellent depending on location.

- Insect repellent — much cheaper than Greece, even though the self-dispensing pharmacies (*farmakío*) are very good.

Making a list of documents in advance
Make sure before you leave that you run through the following list:

- boat registration documents
- copy invoices of personal items being transported
- currency
- driving documents (see Chapter 3)
- ferry tickets *etc*
- form E111
- health insurance certificate
- NHS card
- passport (or identity card)
- student identity card
- travel insurance policy
- visa/permit.

DRIVING YOUR CAR INTO GREECE

This is an area of legislation notoriously inconsistently applied, depending on which authority's advice you seek and which area of Greece you will be driving into. Consider breakdown insurance with the AA or RAC for the duration of the journey – about £85 for 30 days' Europe-wide cover.

Using a tourist's permit
British registered cars may be driven in Greece for a period of six months and are not subject to Customs control. The car registration document and proof of ownership of a caravan or boat will be required. Car owners should at all times be able to prove to the authorities when the car was brought into Greece, and so it is always prudent to keep ferry tickets *etc*, as car details are no longer stamped into passports, and the onus for proving entry dates to Greece is firmly with the car owner. The six month period can be extended, at the discretion of the Customs authorities, for up to a further nine months for which period Greek road

tax is payable. The entitlement to such an extension is strictly personal, consequently only the wife/husband or children may use the car in addition to the owner. After the expiry of the period granted by Customs, the person concerned will be required either to re-export the car or to clear it through Customs. Failure to do so within the valid period may result in Customs imposing fines for each extra day after the expired period. Such fines can be very high.

Keeping the car for a longer period
To qualify for a further period of tax free circulation, either both the car and the owner should be out of Greece for at least 185 days, or the vehicle can remain in Greece provided it is held by Customs for the above period. Most Customs authorities will allow you to use a central car compound for this six months at a nominal daily fee. This 21 month process (15 months' driving followed by six months off the road) can be repeated three times in succession after which either Greek plates should be applied for or the car sold. A word of warning — the Greek authorities are clamping down on British registered cars being driven in Greece for periods longer than the six month tourist's permit. Stories of heavy fines and even of cars being impounded are regularly featured in the Greek media.

Addresses of Customs offices for advice on extensions, transfer or sale of tourist cars in Greece can be found in Useful Addresses.

Checking your driving documents
Drivers in Greece will need a current driving licence. If you have an old, green style UK driving licence, apply for a standard Greek translation, which is free of charge from the Automobile Association, or the Royal Automobile Club (see Useful Addresses). It is also available at the frontier offices. Drivers with EU format licences (pink and more recently pink and green) do not need to carry a translation, nor do drivers with international driving licences. If you hold the latter, remember that it is only valid for one year. Other documents you should have include green card insurance (available from your insurance company or at frontier crossing points) which covers you to drive anywhere in Europe, your V5 registration document (log book) and a GB sticker on display. The Motor Insurers Bureau in Greece (address in Useful Addresses) can help with any queries about driving in Greece.

Applying for a Greek licence
You are entitled to apply for a Greek driving licence without re-taking a

driving test if you want. The application must be made within one year of taking up residence in Greece. A Greek driving licence remains valid until the holder reaches the age of 65 after which an application for extension is required.

Hiring a car

Greece is one of the most expensive countries in Europe in which to hire a car. Try to avoid it. Typically, you should expect to pay from around 100,000 GRD per week in high season for a small Fiat Panda 750cc to around 400,000 GRD per week in high season for a nine seater mini-bus.

People hiring a car or motorcycle in Greece should look carefully into the question of adequate insurance cover. In the event of an accident the driver may be liable for payment of damages and may be held in custody pending payment.

CASE STUDIES

Graham plans to leave

Graham is preparing for end of term and his imminent trip to Greece. He has drawn up a checklist of items to take with him for the eight weeks. Everything appears well planned except that not having been to Greece before Graham is not aware of the effect of mosquitos. When he shows his list of items to his local Greek consulate office, he is advised of the necessity for electric repellent devices. Graham is pleased that he sought professional advice.

Tony and Wendy consider tax

Before Tony and Wendy leave for Greece, they resign from their jobs as teachers, obtaining their P45s accordingly. As they are intent on teaching in Greece, and want to avoid being taxed in both the UK and Greece, they are careful to write to the Inland Revenue advising them of their impending departure dates and making it clear that they will be subject to Greek income tax at local rates, but will declare this income on their UK tax return the following April. The Inland Revenue confirm that double taxation relief is available for UK residents living in Greece.

John and Betty think ahead

Being slightly older and more inclined to worry, John and Betty are anxious that their relatives and friends may not be able to contact them on Skíathos. They are aware that their old cottage has an address albeit descriptive as opposed to practical, but will the postman be able to find them? After telephoning the Greek embassy in London their minds are put to rest when they are given the postal address of the nearest Greek Post Office to their cottage and advised to direct mail for collection to this address using the *poste restante* system, whereby the mail will be held by the Post Office free of charge awaiting their collection.

POINTS TO CONSIDER

1. Draw up a list of all the people and organisations you need to inform of your departure to Greece. Are you sure that you've included everyone?

2. Make a list of all the documents and possessions that you will need to take with you. Think carefully of all your own particular needs. Are you staying for a short term or longer period?

3. Check the weather conditions you are likely to be faced with in Greece. Have you packed the appropriate clothes? Have you thought of all the medical items you will need for the climate and situation?

3

Getting There

Having now made the decision to get up and go, your next move will be to consider how to get yourself and your belongings to Greece, and this will obviously depend on your intentions. Hopefully though, the end result will be as eulogised by John Fowles in his mystery novel *The Magus*, set on the island of Spetses in the 1950s: 'I fell head over heels, totally and for ever in love with the Greek landscape from the moment I arrived.'

NOTING DOWN INITIAL THOUGHTS

A good way of assessing the best way of getting to Greece is to make a list of key questions as follows, and be honest with your answers:

- How long will I be staying in Greece?
- What will the weather be like?
- Am I taking all my worldly possessions with me?
- When do I hope to return?
- Will I be travelling alone?
- What do I need to take with me?
- What is my travel budget?
- Where is my destination?
- Am I taking a car to Greece?

MAKING YOUR WAY TO GREECE

Depending on how much luggage you need to take, you can get to Greece basically in any combination of six ways:

- air
- rail

- bus/coach
- car/motorcycle
- ferries
- hitching.

FLYING FROM BRITAIN

Most of the cheaper flights from Britain to Greece are chartered, which are sold either with a package holiday, or through consolidators as a flight only option. These flights have fixed and changeable outward and return dates, a maximum stay of one month and must meet the somewhat peculiar conditions of Greek law — more on which in the following section.

For longer stays, or more flexibility, or if you are travelling out of season when few charters are available, you will need a scheduled flight. These too are offered under a wide variety of fares, although much more expensive than chartered, and are again often sold off at a discount by consolidators. Examples of a few consolidators specialising in Greece can be found in Useful Addresses.

Although Athens remains the prime destination for cheap fares, there are also direct flights from Britain to Thessaloníkí, Préveza and Kavála on the Greek mainland, Kalamáta on the Peloponnese and to the islands of Crete, Corfu, Hios, Kárpathos, Kefalonía, Kos, Lésvos, Límnos, Míkonos, Páros, Rhodes, Sámos, Santorini, Skíathos, and Zakinthos. Note that some of these airports will be seasonal as many only handle charter flights. With any flight to Athens, you can buy a domestic connecting flight via the national carrier, Olympic, to one of a dozen or so additional Greek mainland and island airports.

The old Athens airport had three terminals: the west terminal handling Olympic Airways flights exclusively (internal and external), the east terminal handling other foreign international flights, and a further charters-only terminal. However, these terminals are now replaced by the new Athens airport at Spata, which opened in the spring of 2001 amidst much national outpouring following considerable delays, cancellations and confusion. The consolidated airport (30 kms northeast of Athens centre) will be able to handle 16,000,000 passengers (internal and external) per annum. The old airport has been closed and will be redeveloped for the Olympic games in 2004.

Taking advantage of charter flights

Some words of warning about Greek aviation law. This specifies that a charter ticket must be a return of no fewer than three days and no more than four weeks, and must be accompanied by an accommodation voucher for at least the first few nights of your stay — check that your ticket satisfies these conditions or you could be refused entry. In practice, the accommodation voucher has become a formality; it has to name an existing hotel, but you are not necessarily expected to use it. As for the time limit, a cheap return flight can often prove advantageous, even just using the outbound half. Examples of a good source of cheap charter tickets can be found in Useful Addresses.

Booking scheduled flights

The advantages of scheduled flights are that they can be booked well in advance, remain valid for three months and sometimes longer, and involve none of the restrictions on charters. As with charters, discount fares on scheduled flights are available from most high street travel agents.

The biggest choice of scheduled flights is with the Greek national carrier, Olympic Airways, which offers the choice of Athens, Thessaloníkí and, depending on season, some of the major island airports. Olympic shares the UK to Athens routes with British Airways and Virgin Airlines. Since the introduction of Virgin to the route in 1994, the other two airlines have had to sharpen their pencil on fare prices, and some extremely good deals are available depending on departure dates.

For maximum flexibility Easy Jet fly a twice-daily service from London Luton to Athens. Inexpensive tickets (£5 discount if booked on the Internet) can be purchased, one-way, therefore enabling you to elect your return date at will. Examples of a few sources for inexpensive scheduled tickets can be found in Useful Addresses.

Pros and cons of scheduled flights

Pros

- Flexibility — tickets can be booked well in advance and remain valid for up to three months.

- Availability — there are numerous flights to Greece each day with a choice of good quality airplanes with the world's leading airlines.

- Guarantees — scheduled flights in the main will leave and arrive on time.

Cons

● Costs — even discounted scheduled tickets can be substantially more expensive than the popular charter tickets.

● Departures — as scheduled flights mainly leave from the larger UK airports, *eg* Heathrow, you may not necessarily be able to fly from your local airport.

● Variety — charter flights being more tourism related are likely to operate direct flights to the islands, whereas the scheduled operators mainly serving business needs primarily fly to the larger towns, *eg* Athens, Thessaloniki.

TRAVELLING BY RAIL

You can now travel through the Eurotunnel, but traditionally the route with British Rail is London to Folkestone on the Hoverspeed and then via Boulogne to Paris which takes just under 20 hours. At Paris you need to catch an 11 hour passage to Bologna in Northern Italy where you have a short wait before catching the onward train to the ferry port at Brindisi, a journey of some ten hours. The evening ferry docks at Pátras on the Greek Peloponnese some 17.5 hours later, leaving you to catch a bus to Athens which rambles along over the Corinth canal, taking about four hours, stopping en route at Corinth for the mandatory 20 minute toilet and *souvláki* (pork kebab) stop.

If you have the time, try and catch the single track Peloponnese narrow gauge train which winds its way from Athens to Kalamata, either via Pátras or Tripolí — a truly memorable journey with spectacular scenery provided it's not too hot.

Using the inter rail

If you intend to travel around Greece, you can buy a 'Freedom' pass in the UK. This entitles you to three, five or ten days travelling in a one month period on the Greek railways.

Travelling as a youth

If you are under the age of 26, you can purchase a special 'two zone' pass for less than £200 which will allow you to travel to and around Greece for a period of up to one month. This is very good value for money. Unfortunately, the snag is that you must be under 26!

Relaxing on the motor rail

Always an expensive option, it is nevertheless possible to have your car transported through France, Switzerland and Italy before crossing the Adriatic sea. Definitely not recommended for those of a nervous financial disposition!

JOURNEYING BY BUS AND COACH

The days of the Magic Bus and other less scrupulous coach operators are over. Spiralling fuel costs have put an end to most of the 'cowboys' who plied their trade between London and Athens, often with insufficient drivers and unsafe coaches.

Nowadays, your best bet is Eurolines. These coaches are operated by National Express with a consortium of the European state bus companies. The route is usually London, Dover, Paris, Rimini, Ancona, Corfu, Igoumenitsa, Pátras and Athens. You will probably need to change coaches in Italy and transfer to a Greek or Italian carrier. Most journeys leave London at about 9:00 a.m. on day one, and reach Athens two days later about midday. Stops of about 20 minutes are made every five or six hours with the odd longer break for roadside cafe meals. You will be able to sleep in peace, safe in the knowledge that three drivers will be working in shifts.

TOURING BY CAR AND MOTORCYCLE

Since the outbreak of war in the former Yugoslavia, the best route from London to Athens has been via Calais, Dijon, Chamonix, Geneva and Milan to Brindisi, then across the Adriatic sea to Igoumenitsa on the Greek mainland and onwards to Athens, a drive of some 2,500 kilometres. However, the increasing cost of the French and Italian road tolls has made this route a bit pricey.

With the introduction of a new ferry service in 1995, the most reasonable route missing out on most of the road tolls is now via Calais, Dunkirk, Lille, Mons, Namur, Luxembourg, Strasbourg, Basel, Luzern, Lugano, Como, Milan, Bologna and to the northern Italian port of Ancona, where a fast ferry service will get you to Pátras on the Greek Peloponnese in only 16 hours. From Pátras, Athens is a little over 160 kilometres away. The total driving route at just over 1,600 kilometres cuts down the traditional journey by some 800 kilometres.

Considering alternate routes

There are an additional three ferry ports in Italy at Venice, Bari and Otranto. Both the Automobile Association and Royal Automobile Club will plot you a journey schedule taking into account your preference for countries to be visited, and views on road tolls and sea crossings. An IBM compatible software programme AutoRoute Europe is available for about £50 which allows you to set your journey parameters and work out the quickest, shortest, preferred and alternative routes for you to consider. Details can be found in Useful Addresses.

Most people allow four days for a relatively leisurely drive down to Greece. If you have time and the idea of a slice of eastern Europe appeals to you, then various routes can be plotted via Hungary, Romania, Bulgaria and Albania.

Motorcycling through Europe

The notion of a leisurely stroll through Europe is very romantic. Unfortunately the French and in particular Italian drivers on the Autostrada do not agree. There are many accidents in Greece, some fatal. The wearing of helmets by motorcyclists is compulsory in Greece — in theory, anyway. The police are empowered to make a fine of 10,000 GRD on any offender they stop.

Remembering your vehicle documents

Take original documents only, photocopies are not allowed. If none is available, then contact the Automobile Association or Royal Automobile Club — details in Useful Addresses.

Taking a letter of authority
If you are taking a vehicle that is not registered in your name, then you will need a letter of authority from the registered keeper to take the car abroad.

Obtaining a green card
As it is almost impossible to get comprehensive insurance in Greece, it is strongly advisable to obtain an international motor insurance certificate (green card). You should discuss this with your insurance company or broker and make sure you apply in plenty of time. The green card 'tops up' insurance cover in Greece to a UK standard.

Getting a vehicle on hire certificate
If you take a hired car or leased private vehicle abroad and cannot obtain

the original vehicle registration document, you will need to take a vehicle on hire certificate (VE103B), available from the motoring organisations.

Driving people carriers
If you are driving a vehicle abroad with more than nine seats, you will find that special documents and tachographs are mandatory. Also, the driver must be over 21 and have at least one full year's driving experience.

Obtaining road maps
Detailed European maps are easy to come by. However, generally speaking the only available Greek maps are those originally drawn up by the military which can be hopelessly inaccurate. Geological maps where available can be a lot better. The Efstathiadis Group in Athens publish a very respectable set of road maps (see Useful Addresses).

Table of Road Tolls in Greece	
	(GRD)
Patrás – Corinth	600
Corinth – Athens	500
Athens – Lamia	750
Lamia – Larissa	500
Larissa – Katerini	500
Katerini – Thessaloniki	500
(Total: Patrás to Thessaloniki	3350
Corinth – Tripoli (Artemission Tunnel)	900

These tolls will increase by up to 300 per cent upon completion of the Patrás to Thessaloniki national road network.

Fig. 4. Road tolls in Greece.

Paying road tolls

All vehicles using the Swiss motorways must display a sticker to show that road tax has been paid for the year. Tax stickers can either be purchased at the borders or from the Swiss National Tourist office in London (see Useful Addresses).

In addition road tolls are payable on an 'as you go' basis in France, Italy, Austria and Greece.

Checking what's needed

As you will be driving through a number of European countries with differing legislation, it is worthwhile to be on the safe side by ensuring you are carrying as many of the following as appropriate:

- appropriate road maps
- beam benders
- fire extinguisher
- first aid kit
- full set of up to date maps
- GB sticker
- green card insurance
- international driving licence (if necessary)
- schedule of personal belongings being transported
- snow chains
- spare set of bulbs
- translation of driving licence (if necessary)
- UK/EU driving licence
- V5 car registration document
- V561 certificate of export
- vehicle on hire certificate
- vehicle sales invoice
- warning triangle.

CROSSING ON THE FERRIES

The Dover/Folkestone to Calais, and Ramsgate to Dunkirk/Ostend ferries have always been the most popular way of crossing the Channel. With the opening of the Eurotunnel between Folkestone and Calais, you can now turn up at the ferry port and, subject to no queuing time, be in France in just over half an hour.

New technology also enables a swift crossing of the Adriatic sea. In only 20 hours you can now get from Ancona in northern Italy to Pátras on the Greek Peloponnese, saving approximately 16 hours from the previous ship timetable. The new crossing reduces the driving distance considerably to 1,800 kilometres and includes a mini-cruise as well!

The best agency to book your English Channel and Adriatic sea crossings with is probably Viamare Travel Ltd, who act as the UK General Sales Agents for most of the ferry operators and offer reasonable discount prices for booking all your travel arrangements together. Details of ferry operators in Useful Addresses.

HITCHING DOWN TO GREECE

The best plan for hitchers is to talk yourself into a lift on the ferry across to France or Belgium. A sympathetic truck driver might offer a single lift most of the way to Italy or Hungary. The Channel ports are hopeless places to hitch out of. Try and avoid hitching through France, as the French are amongst the worst in Europe for stopping.

CASE STUDIES

Graham buys the cheapest ticket

Young Graham, our university student friend, decides to travel to Greece as cheaply as possible. He buys a one-way coach ticket from an agent advertising in *Time Out* magazine at the remarkable price of just £70. He boards the modern air-conditioned coach at London Victoria and travels on the Dover to Calais ferry only to find at the French ferry port that the coach for the onward journey is an old beaten up bus that has obviously seen better days. Not only that, the promise of three drivers back in England has now evaporated to one, with the promise maybe of a second driver when they reach Italy! Graham learns the hard way that cheapest isn't always best.

Tony and Wendy fall foul of the authorities

Tony and Wendy travel to Greece in their camper van. They choose the quickest route from London to Athens in order to save on overnight accommodation. In total, they drive just over 1,900 trouble free kilometres except for one problem which gets them into hot water with the Swiss police authorities: they forgot to apply to the Swiss National Tourist Office in London for their *vignette* temporary tax disc providing one year's free motoring on the Swiss motorway system. They could have bought one at the German/Swiss border, but as they were oblivious to the need, they drive until stopped and fined by a vigilant Swiss policeman.

John gets registered

John and Betty decide to enjoy their retirement by flying direct from Gatwick to Skíathos to start work renovating their lovely old cottage. Upon arriving in Greece, John visits his local IKA office and hands over his health form E111 in exchange for a medical booklet. He is directed to a doctor who works for the social insurance scheme, for which there is no charge. However, upon his first visit he is informed that the *farmakéo* (chemist) will charge him an additional 25 per cent of any prescription costs for drugs.

POINTS TO CONSIDER

1. Plan your route to Greece as carefully as possible. Are you sure you've double-checked timetables, currencies needed, costs of road tolls *etc* with the latest available information?

2. Have you worked out the cost of road tolls payable in France and Italy? Would this money together with the savings on fuel be greater than the additional cost of buying a longer sea crossing — say Ancona to Pátras?

3. Look carefully at the cost of charter flights versus scheduled flights. Last minute bargains to be found in the national press sometimes favour scheduled flights due to their greater availability and regularity.

4

Where to Stay

Greece and its kaleidoscope of culture, language and people is a fascinating proposition. In the words of Dr Johnson, 'Greek, sir, is like lace: every man gets as much of it as he can.' Your decision where to live will be based on a mixture of family, friends, work opportunities and natural love of the area.

CHOOSING WHERE TO LIVE

Greece has always been plagued by earthquakes, mostly minor, the most recent significant movement being in September 1999 which left 150 dead and scores of buildings destroyed in the Attica region. In this instance the Government quickly set up a code of severity, marking affected properties with either a green, yellow or red painted cross. Green depicted the 'all clear' no damage noted, yellow reflected cosmetic damage for which the owners could claim a restoration grant of 200,000 GRD towards repairs (with an additional interest free loan for 15 years if needed) and red, as the colour suggests, indicated dangerous and appropriate for demolition. It is well worth taking geography into account as well as how long you intend to stay and what your longer term plans are, and in this respect you should sit down with a map of Greece and consider some of the following questions:

- How happy am I with a very hot, dry and polluted climate such as in Athens? Would I prefer a more temperate climate in the country?

- What are the advantages and disadvantages of living near the sea?

- Could I handle the semi-isolation of living on an island, especially in the winter when the domestic airports are closed and rough weather forces the ferries to stop?

● How important is accessibility to an international airport? How often do I need to fly back to the UK?

● What sort of work am I after — seasonal (olive picking *etc*) or more permanent, where larger cities provide the opportunities?

The National Tourist Office of Greece in London (NTOG) will readily forward you specific information on each region you may be interested in. See Useful Addresses for details.

WHAT ACCOMMODATION IS AVAILABLE?

Once you have worked out in your mind the region of Greece which best suits your working conditions, you should next consider the type of accommodation most appropriate to you, which can be sub-divided as:

● temporary
● short term rental
● longer term stay
● purchase.

Seeking temporary accommodation

If you are a student or casual traveller and not sure of your longer term intentions, there are a number of options, without commitment, to provide a roof over your head whilst allowing you to move on at a moment's notice. Some temporary forms of accommodation to consider are:

● camping
● youth hostels
● hotels.

Going to an organised campsite

Camping in Greece is only permitted on organised sites. You will find that the tourist police, especially on the islands, are keen to restrict camping and caravanning to authorised areas. There are over 20 authorised sites on the Attica mainland, some open all year round. Rates vary depending on season, facilities and location.

ΕΛΛΗΝΙΚΟΣ ΟΡΓΑΝΙΣΜΟΣ ΤΟΥΡΙΣΜΟΥ
HELLENIC TOURISM ORGANISATION

ΠΙΝΑΚΙΔΑ ΕΝΗΜΕΡΩΣΗΣ ΤΟΥ ΠΕΛΑΤΗ - GUEST INFORMATION

ΞΕΝΟΔΟΧΕΙΟ
HOTEL .... Ακροπολις ...... Παρμα ...... ΤΑΞΗ CLASS E1

ΑΡΙΘ.ΔΩΜΑΤΙΟΥ ΜΕ/ΧΩΡΙΣ ΛΟΥΤΡΟ Η ΝΤΟΥΣ ..5.9.... ΑΡΙΘ.ΚΛΙΝΩΝ ..2..
ROOM WITH/WITHOUT BATH OR SHOWER .....5.9.... No OF BEDS ..2..

ΑΠΟ FROM	ΕΩΣ ΤΟ	ΑΠΟ FROM	ΕΩΣ ΤΟ	ΑΠΟ FROM	ΕΩΣ ΤΟ	
1/1	30/6	1/7	31/8	1/9	31/12	
DRS ―		DRS ―		DRS ―		ΤΙΜΗ ΚΛΙΜΑΤΙΖΟΜΕΝΟΥ ΔΩΜΑΤΙΟΥ RATE OF AIR-CONDITIONED ROOM
DRS 3,300		DRS 6,600		DRS 3,300		ΤΙΜΗ ΔΩΜΑΤΙΟΥ ΧΩΡΙΣ ΚΛΙΜΑΤΙΣΜΟ ROOM RATE WITHOUT A/C
DRS ―		DRS ―		DRS ―		ΤΙΜΗ ΠΡΩΪΝΟΥ ΚΑΤ'ΑΤΟΜΟ BREAKFAST PER PERSON
DRS ―		DRS ―		DRS ―		ΤΙΜΗ ΓΕΥΜΑΤΟΣ Η ΔΕΙΠΝΟΥ ΚΑΤ'ΑΤΟΜΟ TABLE D'HÔTE LUNCH OR DINNER PER PERSON

Ο ΔΙΕΥΘΥΝΤΗΣ ΤΟΥ ΞΕΝΟΔΟΧΕΙΟΥ
THE HOTEL MANAGER

ΣΤΙΣ ΠΑΡΑΠΑΝΩ ΤΙΜΕΣ ΣΥΜΠΕΡΙΛΑΜΒΑΝΟΝΤΑΙ ΟΛΕΣ ΟΙ ΕΠΙΒΑΡΥΝΣΕΙΣ ALL CHARGES ARE INCLUDED ON THE ABOVE ROOM RATES
Η ΛΗΨΗ ΤΟΥ ΠΡΩΪΝΟΥ ΕΙΝΑΙ/ΔΕΝ ΕΙΝΑΙ ΥΠΟΧΡΕΩΤΙΚΗ
BREAKFAST IS/IS NOT OBLIGATORY
Η ΛΗΨΗ ΤΗΣ ΗΜΙΔΙΑΤΡΟΦΗΣ ΕΙΝΑΙ/ΔΕΝ ΕΙΝΑΙ ΥΠΟΧΡΕΩΤΙΚΗ
HALF BOARD IS/IS NOT OBLIGATORY

ΠΡΟΣΑΥΞΗΣΗ/INCREASE
ΓΙΑ ΠΑΡΑΜΟΝΗ ΜΕΧΡΙ ΔΥΟ ΗΜΕΡΩΝ ΠΡΟΣΤΙΘΕΤΑΙ 10% ΣΤΗ ΤΙΜΗ ΔΩΜΑΤΙΟΥ
FOR A STAY UP TO TWO DAYS A 10% IS TO BE ADDED ON THE ROOM RATE

ΣΗΜΕΙΩΣΗ/NOTE
ΠΕΡΙΣΣΟΤΕΡΕΣ ΠΛΗΡΟΦΟΡΙΕΣ ΓΙΑ ΤΙΣ ΤΙΜΕΣ ΑΝΑΓΡΑΦΟΝΤΑΙ ΣΤΗΝ ΣΧΕΤΙΚΗ ΠΙΝΑΚΙΔΑ ΠΟΥ ΕΙΝΑΙ ΑΝΑΡΤΗΜΕΝΗ ΣΤΟ ΧΩΡΟ ΥΠΟΔΟΧΗΣ ΤΟΥ ΞΕΝΟΔΟΧΕΙΟΥ.
PLEASE FIND MORE INFORMATION ON ROOM RATES ON THE BOARD POSTED AT THE RECEPTION DESK

ΘΕΩΡΗΘΗΚΕ
ISSUED IN THE ...... 29. 3. /199.9

Fig. 5. Hotel tariff card.

Risking illegal camping
Freelance camping outside authorised camp sites is such an established element of Greek travel that few people realise that it is officially forbidden. Since 1977, however, it has been forbidden by law and increasingly the regulations are enforced. If you do camp freelance therefore it is vital to exercise sensitivity and discretion. Obviously the Greek authorities crack down on people camping rough and dropping litter near popular tourist beaches. They get especially concerned when a large community of campers start descending. Off the beaten track, however, and particularly in rural inland areas nobody is very concerned. Wherever you are, it is always best to ask permission locally in the village *kafenío* before pitching a tent.

Pinpointing youth hostels
If you are a member of the international Youth Hostels Association, you will be eligible to stay at any of the three hostels in Athens or the one in Piraeus. Otherwise you can ask for an international guest card at the Greek Youth Hostel headquarters – details in Useful Addresses.

Also providing inexpensive accommodation are the YMCA (*XAN*) and the YWCA (*XEN*), both of which are open for most of the year. Once again, the NTOG can provide details.

Checking in at hotels
In the Athens area alone there are more than 160 hotels and boarding houses, ranging from the super luxury class to modest rooms in private homes. It is a good idea to book in advance during the summer months. Those who arrive without reservations should contact the Greek Chamber of Hotels at the airport to find a room. A similar office is open until 8 pm in the National Tourist Organisation's central information office – see Useful Addresses. Failing that you can call the tourist police on 171 who speak English.

Regulating hotel prices
Prices are controlled according to a category list compiled by NTOG. Note however, that deluxe or luxury establishments are not listed. Hotels are graded from luxury class (L) through first to fifth class (A-E). Room prices are usually displayed on bedroom doors — see Figure 5. Prices in most cases are per room, and a 15 per cent service charge is normally included in the bill. When you arrive at your hotel, you will be asked to fill in a registration form and your passport may be kept overnight. The more modest hotels might not accept credit card payment, and you should not be surprised

if you are asked to pay for a room in advance. Most hotels quote for a double room with bath but without breakfast. You will find that tariffs range from 4,000–5,000 GRD for a modest class 'E' room for the night to well over 85,000 GRD for a palatial suite in a class 'A' hotel. You will be expected to leave your room by noon on the day of departure.

Finding shorter term rentals

While you are looking for permanent accommodation you could stay in a pension, or even with a family. Contact any tourist office (*touristiko grafió*) or travel office (*taxidiotika grafió*) for local availability and further information.

Considering pensions

Accommodation of this kind in small hotels or private houses can be very good. The standards are controlled and graded by the NTOG, but take each one on its own merit and inspect before you commit yourself. At best they are very good with private bathroom facilities.

Booking rooms

In the main tourist areas, there are generally plenty of private houses offering rooms (*domátio*) at budget rates. If you arrive in Greece by ferry, the chances are that you will be met at the dockside by a cluster of 'rooms to let' notices, otherwise enquire at the local National Tourist Office of Greece or with the tourist police.

This form of accommodation is officially controlled and divided into three classes (A-C). They are usually cheaper than hotels and are in general spotlessly clean. In these days, the bulk of them are in new purpose-built low rise blocks, but some are in people's homes where you will occasionally be treated to fabulous hospitality.

Inspecting the facilities

At its simplest, the room will be clean but basic and toilet facilities (cold water only) outside in the courtyard. At best it could be a modern fully furnished place with an en suite bathroom. Between these two extremes you may well find a well-appointed kitchen and a choice of rooms at various prices. In winter, private rooms are closed pretty well universally to keep the hotels in business.

Over the years it has now become standard practice for landlords to ask to keep your passport, ostensibly for the tourist police, but in reality to prevent you leaving without paying.

Staying in student houses
In Athens there are a number of cheap dormitory style student houses, non YHA hostels which despite their names are in no way committed to students. Conditions are in general fairly basic, but if you are on your own, the prices you are likely to get will be about the best in town.

Living with a family
For young people in particular, the comfort of staying with a family with at least one English speaking member is ideal. You will soon get to learn the Greek culture, perhaps learn some of the language — especially if you are involved in family visits. You will find that the wider Greek family will take you to their hearts very quickly and there will be much smiling, laughing and genial conversation which you will need to sit through and enjoy until you start to understand.

The Greeks spend far more time with their families than we do in the UK and indeed most of the weekend may be spent visiting and delivering small presents.

Pros and cons of staying with a family

Pros:

● great if you can fit in with the Greek life style
● friendly way to explore the area and meet people
● excellent way to learn the language.

Cons:

● you may not get a key to the door
● compliance with family rules on staying out late *etc*
● you may not get on with all members of the family.

Looking for longer term rentals
Real Estate Agents in Athens can help find accommodation to rent, although a fee is normally paid by the lessee. Details can be found in the Greek telephone directory, equivalent of our *Yellow Pages* (*Chryssos Odigos*).

Houses, flats and out of season villas are often rented by the week or month. If you have two or three people to share costs and want to stay on an island or a mainland coastal resort for a while it is an option well worth considering.

Exchanging your home
Exchanging your home in the UK for one in Greece for a contract period is potentially an excellent way of solving your accommodation needs while in Greece. Clearly, it is important to draw up Heads of Agreement which state the conditions and collaterals that will be required. Relevant Greek organisations to contact can be found in Useful Addresses.

FINDING A PLACE TO RENT

As soon as you are settled in Greece and get to understand the area that you are proposing to live and work in, the best way to find semi-permanent accommodation is:

● At a *períptero* — there is now a newspaper specifically for renting apartments and houses.

● By word of mouth in local bars, *kafenío etc*

● Keep your eyes open in the local newspapers.

● Pay a visit to the local tourist office (*touristiko grafíó*).

● Visit a real estate agency, although most are concerned with sales and purchase only.

● Walk the area looking for the 'to let' (*enikiazete*) signs on doors *etc*.

Considering apartments
Both furnished and unfurnished accommodation is available. Property to rent is advertised in the newspaper under the heading '*enikiassis akiniton*'. The usual deposit needed for rented accommodation is equivalent to two months' rent. Rental contracts are usually for two years, and sometimes even longer.

There is always a considerable number of apartments scattered around popular tourist locations. Many are in the hands of letting agencies who place them with tour operators. One method for searching them out is to read through the holiday brochures of companies which specialise in this type of accommodation. Many of these villas are often not in use until late May or early June, so it is possible to come to a private arrangement usually at very attractive rates.

BUYING A PROPERTY

Caveat emptor — let the buyer beware! This can be a complex legal process which should not be undertaken lightly. Expert legal advice should always be sought before entering into contractual terms. Having said that, the whole operation can work remarkably smoothly once you know the ropes.

Foreigners may purchase property in Greece. Recent changes in Greek law now permit foreign ownership of property in previously sensitive areas such as Crete and Corfu. There are few UK type estate agents, but a growing number of property consultants. The best people to approach for advice and assistance on this subject are multi-lingual lawyers. The British embassy has a list of Greek lawyers who correspond in English. UK publications such as *International Property Times*, *Homes Abroad* and the overseas property section of the leading national broadsheets, *eg Sunday Times*, have specialist sections advertising overseas property.

A few specialist agencies in the UK and Greece have sprung up over the last few years offering very good advice and introductory services. Useful Addresses lists a few that advertise regularly.

Building your own place

Housing in Greece is privately owned, and whilst the choice is enormous, including luxury villas on the islands and in the suburbs of Athens, the problem is that Greeks rarely sell their homes, preferring instead to build another level to accommodate the next generation and then pass the house on when they die.

Land is in short supply and in high demand. Land areas are often expressed as *stremmatta*, which is 1,000 square metres or roughly a quarter of an acre. If you do find land for sale there will nearly always be an architect nearby who will provide a design and build contract. Greek completion dates vary wildly with our understanding and timing of 'finished'. A good commercial contract drawn up by a bilingual lawyer is imperative. Don't skimp on this cost.

Understanding the regulations for acquisition

Generally, as previously stated, there are no restrictions on non-residents acquiring real estate in Greece even in the border areas. However, both EU and non EU residents must obtain permission from the appropriate authorities before purchasing real estate in border areas. Once you have purchased your property, you become the freehold owner in perpetuity.

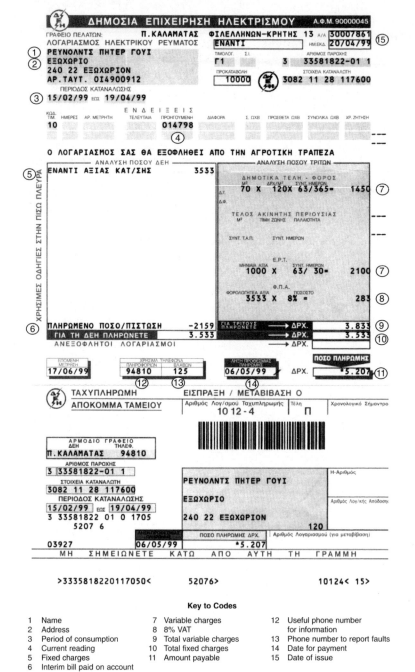

Fig. 6. Utilities bill.

Key to Codes

1	Name	7	Variable charges	12	Useful phone number
2	Address	8	8% VAT		for information
3	Period of consumption	9	Total variable charges	13	Phone number to report faults
4	Current reading	10	Total fixed charges	14	Date for payment
5	Fixed charges	11	Amount payable	15	Date of issue
6	Interim bill paid on account				

56

Looking at the annual outgoings

At present there are no recurring rates or taxes on homes in Greece other than a nominal mains water charge and the cost of waste removal and street cleaning, which are included within the four monthly electricity bill (see Figure 6). You will need to contact the local office of the relevant national company for details of supply. The national electricity company is *Dimmossia Steria Ilektrismou* (DEH). The national telecommunications company is *Organismos Telepikinonion Ellados* (OTE). A municipal gas company has been set up for Athens; however, the first connections are yet to be made as the network is still under construction. Contact your local town hall (*dimarchio*) in Greece for details of water supply. Water bills are raised annually in the country and every three months in the larger towns and cities.

Following the system

Bearing in mind that property is expensive, largely due to its limited availability, you really should start off by finding a bilingual agent who knows the area well.

In the past, when Greece suffered from spiralling inflation, mortgages were rare with rates commonly charged at around 30 per cent. Nowadays, as Greece prepares to join the EMU, and headline inflation needs to be governed, loans to buy property are available in the region of 7 to 10 per cent.

Getting involved with the purchasing procedures

The first stage in the conveyancing is to sign a Sales Agreement and pay a deposit — usually 10 per cent. This agreement contains the names of the parties, a description of the property, the price, the method of payment and any special conditions negotiable in the purchase process.

The vendor will then be instructed to take the property off the market whilst your appointed lawyer completes the purchase transaction. Under Greek law, no contract is enforceable unless it is in writing, It is important therefore that once an offer has been made and accepted all purchase documents are checked by a lawyer before signing to ensure that the vendor has rightful title to the property.

Losing your deposit

If you do not go ahead with buying the property after you have paid your deposit, you will forfeit it and face potential legal action from the vendor. However, if the vendor pulls out of the deal after receiving your deposit, you are entitled to claim a return of double the deposit in compensation. The compensation will not affect your statutory rights to legal action against the vendor for breach of contract.

Finding the experts
You will undoubtedly need a good team of four and a fair amount of patience:

- bilingual agent
- notary public
- lawyer
- banker.

Liaising with an agent
The agent will normally barter the purchase consideration on your behalf. If you choose to attend this ritual, be prepared for a long duration as the relevant merits of the family, the property, the village/town *etc* are proudly promoted by the seller. When the shenanigans are finally over, and a price is agreed upon, the *oúzo* and *mezédhes* will appear and suddenly everyone will be part of one large happy family, with promises of much merriment and rejoicing. The agent, in co-ordinating the purchase process, is also likely to establish via the lawyer who the owners are of the adjoining properties. The boundaries are then fixed by topographical survey. Such a survey carried out by an expert could cost in the region of £100.

Appointing a Notary Public
Your first experience of this official will be the visit together with your agent to sign your Sale Agreement using the Greek bible as the swearing oath. The Notary Public works with your lawyer to ensure that the contracts are drawn up in an orderly fashion and presented to the taxation authorities on time. Before any transaction takes place, your lawyer will carry out searches with the Land Registry. The Notary Public will not proceed with a contract concerning a property which does not have a clean title, free of mortgage obligations *etc*. You will normally be expected to pay a fee of up to 1.6 per cent of the 'notional value' of the property as recorded in the Contract of Sale.

Finding a lawyer
A good, English speaking, well qualified conveyance solicitor is absolutely essential. Although some addresses can be found in the Useful Addresses section, word of mouth is best, and you will probably

be introduced to a recommended lawyer by your agent, who will probably have already established a working relationship from previous purchase negotiations. The lawyer will draw up the Contract of Sale on your behalf, in Greek, arrange the signing ceremony with the vendors, normally at the office of the local Notary Public, and also negotiate the purchase tax with the local taxation office. You should allow 1-1.5 per cent of the purchase price for this service.

Getting a banker
The vendor will probably require payment in sterling or deutschmarks. You will have opened a drachma and also sterling account in preparation at either a private or national bank. Normally, your bank will arrange to pay the vendor a ten per cent deposit at point of signing contracts and allow a further 30 days for the remaining consideration to be settled, although the settlement period can vary per transaction. Your choice of banker will depend on day to day considerations such as location, connection with UK banks, opening hours *etc*.

Working out the taxes to be paid

Generally, depending on local conditions, you should expect to pay two taxes:

- purchase tax
- stamp duty.

Evaluating purchase tax
This is a moving target, payable to the Greek Inland Revenue to cover property transfers. In reality it is levied between 9-13 per cent of the purchase consideration, depending on the negotiating skills of your lawyer and which side of the bed the taxation official got out of. Theoretically, on plots of land you pay between 9-11 per cent and on apartments and houses 11-13 per cent as in Figure 7.

Table of Property Purchase Tax		
Assessed property value	*Plots of land*	*Houses and apartments*
0–4,000,000 GRD	9%	11%
4,000,000 GRD and over	11%	13%

Fig. 7. Property purchase tax.

The real issue is that of 'notional value'. Your lawyer will argue that the real value of the property is much lower than that actually paid, and accordingly the purchase tax percentage should be paid on a lower base. This apparently irrational logic is well-versed, and adds up to part of the service you are paying your lawyer for.

Declaring a value

The 'declared' value will usually amount to about two thirds of the true purchase price, reducing the profit on sale by the vendor (thereby reducing the Greek capital gains tax) and of course reducing the purchase tax and stamp duty payable by the purchaser. Don't forget, this is all well and good until you come to sell the property — your 'base cost' will be less than you actually paid for the property, therefore the apparent profit on sale will be greater with a resultant higher capital gains tax amount payable. Swings and roundabouts! You will need to accompany your lawyer to the tax office to complete final signatures, unless you give your agent 'power of attorney' to sign on your behalf.

In larger cities the tax payable is based on current valuation rates of the tax authorities which are published and known in advance. The Greek Inland Revenue will base their assessment on these special tables issued by the Ministry of Finance. These tables determine the value of the property, *ie* location, quality of construction *etc*. Out in the country, and on the islands the value will be discussed and determined among the local elder statesmen.

Calculating stamp duty

Approximately three per cent of the purchase tax will be added to the overall amount of government taxation payable. Note the three per cent is levied on the purchase tax, not on the purchase price.

LETTING YOUR PROPERTY

As you would expect, there is a huge demand for properties to let, especially on the islands. Letting your property to friends, or advertising in the Sunday newspapers, are by far the best approaches. You could consider packaging a bundle to include flight and car hire, especially if your property is away from the more popular or accessible points. A concise handbook on the property, area and people to contact if things go wrong is always a good idea.

Alternatively, if you are looking for a guaranteed rental income, you should approach a specialist Greek tour operator who would take over total responsibility for letting, cleaning and maintaining your property for a contract period. Details of such agencies are in Useful Addresses.

SELLING YOUR PROPERTY

Sales of foreign owned property in Greece are rare. You would probably initially wish either to advertise details in the UK's specialist publications (*Homes Abroad, Sunday Times* property section *etc*) or to entrust a bilingual agent to promote the property locally.

Handling the sales proceeds
The sales consideration is subject to capital gains tax in the UK on the profit made. It is probably best to arrange for your purchaser to remit funds in sterling to a nominated UK bank account. Make sure that you obtain an official import document (pink slip). Many transactions are conveyed at the Greek embassy in London with purchase monies being freely transferred in sterling in this country. Once again expert legal advice is strongly advisable.

CASE STUDIES

Graham finds a monastery
Graham is determined to live life to the full and see as much of Greece as he can in the eight week summer vacation. He is aware of the location of youth hostels and the recognised camping sites, but he is intent on visiting Mount Athos, on the Halkidhikí peninsula, near Thessaloniki, where he assumes accommodation will be limited. He asks at a local *kafenío* for a place to stay and then sets about finding out more about the 20 monasteries on the mountainside, known as the Monks Republic — the male-only autonomous part of Greece. Unfortunately as he needs to apply in advance for a visa from Thessaloniki to stay on Mount Athos he is unable to get further.

Tony and Wendy get into trouble
Tony and Wendy drive their camper van through Europe arriving in Greece via Italy tired and hungry. As soon as they have cleared Customs they vow to find the first scenic spot overlooking the sea, have a dip, cook a meal and settle down for the night. Unfortunately, the secluded pine grove just off the road is not far enough out of sight of the local tourist police. In the middle of cooking their meal, they are informed

that their mobile gas cooker is a fire risk, and that an overnight stay is illegal. With a certain amount of ill feeling they pack their belongings away, and move on to the recognised local camp site advised by the tourist police. They find out the hard way that the tourist police are vigilant about forbidden camping.

John and Betty pay the price

John and Betty had already purchased the old stone cottage on their idyllic island of Skíathos some 12 months earlier, and they think that all the formalities are complete. However, upon reaching Skíathos they are contacted by their resident agent who informs them that there is still an outstanding matter the taxation authorities wish to discuss. Together with their English speaking lawyer they visit the local tax office, where they are informed that post-completion a small tax remains unpaid. All parties appear puzzled, but there is no option but to pay the additional taxation levied which can be back-dated up to five years, in order to finalise the paperwork. Things happen in Greece that quite often are as much a surprise to the English speaking experts as they are to the visitors!

POINTS TO CONSIDER

1. Think of the winter. All accommodation looks good with the sun on it, but does the roof leak? Are you prepared to be cut off on an island by bad weather?

2. Are you prepared to learn Greek? If not, stay nearer the larger cities with a more accepted cosmopolitan way of life. Nevertheless, the Greeks truly appreciate any effort to learn what they accept is a difficult language. The easiest way to make friends is to develop the basic sentences and learn the everyday greetings and small talk.

3. Don't rush in. Spend some time in the region and town of your choice. You should perhaps consider renting a property for a year or several months before you look to purchase. At least you will have a clear idea of the advantages and disadvantages of the area and the local politics — it is easy to offend unwittingly and suffer the consequences later.

5

Settling In

Greece is renowned for its bureaucracy: a member state of the EU in name but very eastern in some aspects of its culture and dealings with foreigners. Having said that, provided you are able to set aside the time to queue endlessly, and prepared to move from department to department, then the whole process really is very logical, albeit extremely time consuming and frustrating — and it must be pursued personally. You will find that a lot of government personnel seem to be confused with their own rules!

REGISTERING YOUR ARRIVAL

As we have discussed earlier, in order to live and work in Greece you must have a full UK/EU passport. You are free to enter Greece for up to three months to look for work or to set up your business. Don't forget, even if you are visiting Greece to look for work, you may be asked to prove that you have adequate finances for the duration of your stay and that you have the money to pay for a return ticket. Greece is trying to crack down on its vagrant population. There are no specific figures available for those who are 'hiding' and those who are not. It is estimated that there are currently 500,000 illegal immigrants living in Greece; 90 per cent of those come from East Europe.

Applying for a residence permit

If you are working or looking for work but intend to be in Greece for less than three months, then you will need to register with the local police station (*astinomía*) within eight days of arrival. If you intend to stay longer than three months then a residence permit will be needed. A temporary permit is issued in the case of employment lasting for more than three months and less than twelve. Permits are issued for six months in the first instance, and then renewed for a five year period. You must produce your passport, a letter of intent of employment (or proof

63

that financially you can support yourself) and a medical certificate stating that you are free from diseases *etc*. Medical certificates can be obtained from a local hospital. All permits are available from local police stations or, if within Athens, the Aliens Department (*Ipiresía Allodhapón*) — details in Useful Addresses.

Contacting the British Consul

You should register your arrival and current address in Greece with your nearest British consulate as soon as you arrive. In the case of emergencies they will be the first point of communication for friends or family in the UK.

SEEKING HEALTH TREATMENT

You will be receiving health services from the Social Insurance Institute (IKA). Be prepared to face long waits in its offices, surgeries and hospitals. Wards are likely to be crowded and may not provide all the services usual in other EU countries. If you are charged for any services make sure you obtain a receipt with a number perforated across it.

Finding doctors and dentists

Take your E111 and passport to the local IKA office, where you will be given a health services book, and directed to the nearest IKA clinic, doctor or dentist in the scheme. Consultations and treatment are free. However, you will have to pay a proportion of the cost of secondary examinations, *eg* X-rays. You will also have to pay for supplementary treatment like physiotherapy, as well as for dentures.

For prescribed medicines, take the prescription and the health services book to any IKA accredited chemist. You will have to pay a small notional charge, plus 25 per cent of the actual cost of the medicine, which is non-refundable. If you are charged in full, obtain a receipt and ask for the prescription back. Keep the self-adhesive labels from the medicines and stick these on the prescription, you will not get a refund without them.

Getting approval for admittance to hospital

Following the doctor's diagnosis you must request a 'ticket', which is your authorisation to attend hospital. If you go into hospital without the 'ticket' you must show the receptionist your E111, and ask them to contact the IKA office on your behalf. If you obtain medicines or any kind of treatment privately, you must pay the full cost. In these instances return to the IKA office with the receipts, E111 and health services book within four weeks. You will be reimbursed up to the limit allowed for similar treatment by IKA.

Be careful if you are staying in a rural area of Greece, or a small island – there may be no local IKA office. In those circumstances you have no option but to pay the cost of private treatment in full and apply for a refund on return to the UK.

FINDING YOUR WAY AROUND THE SYSTEM

The beauty of Greece is that the organisation is very simple and laid back, which is perhaps why it is not the most efficient in the world, but don't believe that the system works all the time.

Getting your bearings

In the larger cities you should find a tourist organisation (*Organismós Tourismóu*) that will have either a map of the town or at least a list of the major banks, post offices, museums, archaeological sites *etc*. As with all foreign travel, word of mouth is your best source of information. Failing that, a trip to the local British consulate office should provide you with English language leaflets.

Understanding the postal system

The post office (*tachidromío*) normally opens on weekdays between 7.30 am and 2 pm, although in the larger cities they may well close at 8 pm and also stay open on a Saturday. The cost of a stamp (*grammatósima*) to send letters and postcards to Europe is currently 170 GRD and to the USA 250 GRD. The post boxes are the yellow square tin objects mostly found at waist height on telegraph poles *etc*. If you are confronted by a post box with two slots, *esoterikó* is for local mail and *exoterikó* for over-seas. Post offices offer currency exchange at low rates of commission.

Sending mail and parcels

Air mail letters from the mainland take three to six days to reach the rest of Europe. Allow an extra four to five days when sending from any island. Postcards can be extremely slow, up to two weeks for Europe. A fee of about 600 GRD for express service (*katapígonda*) to Europe and 700 GRD to the USA will usually cut delivery time by a few days to any destination.

As the cost of sending postcards and envelopes (*fakellos*) are the same, if you put postcards into envelopes and send air mail, this will

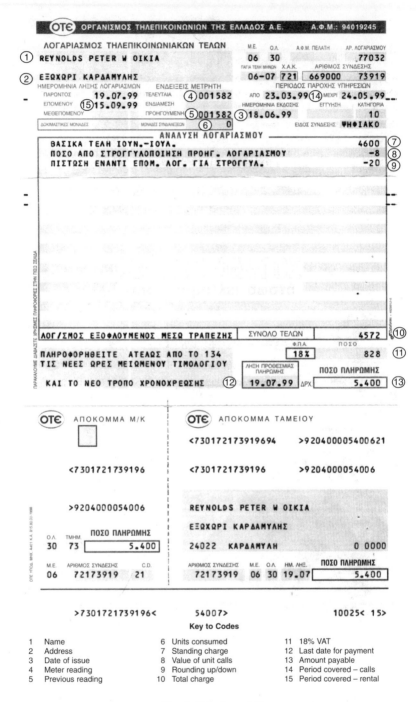

Fig. 8. Telephone bill.

reduce the journey time by about a week. Registered (*sistiméno*) delivery is also available, but once again is quite slow unless coupled with express service. Stamps (*grammatósima*) can also be purchased at a *períptero* (corner kiosk). However, a small quirk of the Greek system is that the proprietors are entitled to add a ten per cent commission for their service.

If you are sending large parcels home, note that they quite often can only be handled in sizeable towns. The post office clerk is obliged to check the contents of any registered letters as well as parcels addressed to foreign destinations, so don't seal this kind of mail until it has been approved.

Receiving mail
Until you have found a permanent or semi-permanent address all mail should be clearly addressed and marked *poste restante* with your surname underlined to the main post office of whichever town you choose. It will be held for a month and you will need your passport to collect it.

Making telephone calls
You are welcome to make calls from hotel receptions, street cafes (*kafenío*) and corner kiosks (*períptero*) in addition to local telephone booths. Booths with a blue band on top are for local (*topikó*) calls; those with an orange strip are intended for long distance (*iperastikó*) and international calls. Don't forget, if you call from a hotel you should expect a hefty surcharge, sometimes up to 50 per cent. Watch out for the standard phone response of *bros* which means 'who's there?' Card phones are now available in many areas and will gradually replace the coin operated telephones.

Keeping the costs down
The advantage of making calls from a *períptero etc* is that the phone is connected to a meter and you pay the exact cost after you have made the call. The days have gone of local inter-state calls costing just 10 GRD for unlimited talk time. Long distance national calls in particular are now very dear which makes Greece one of the most expensive countries in Europe to telephone from, especially as the reliability of the telephone system cannot be guaranteed. You will generally have to try a number of times to get through.

If you need to make an international call it is less expensive to do so from the OTE (*Organismós Telepikiníon tis Elladhós*). The international code for England is 0044 then ignore the leading 0 of the domestic number. Overseas calls will cost very approximately 100 GRD per minute to all EU countries and the rest of Europe. Cheap rates, such as they are, apply from 3-5 pm and 9 pm to 8 am daily plus all weekends for calls within Greece. There is a very small discount for international calls after 10 pm dialled from the mainland only.

Installing a telephone
This is a dream for many people. Quite often, and especially in the remoter towns and villages, there can be a considerable wait for new lines to be installed, unless someone has two lines and is perhaps willing to sell one to you. Otherwise, the official cost of having a line put in is about 45,000 GRD. Mobile phones are instantly available in larger towns of course, but check on quality of reception before purchase — insist on an initial trial or hire for say a week before committing yourself. According to a recent article in *Athens News*, around half the adults in Greece now own a mobile phone.

Surfing the internet
There are three main service providers in Greece: Forthnet, OTEnet and Internet Hellas. You will need a PC and minimum 56k bandwidth modem. Subscription costs are around 13,000 GRD for three months, 25,000 GRD for six months or 47,000 GRD for 12 months. Access calls to the Internet server cost 120 GRD per hour during the day and 60 GRD 'off peak' from 10 pm. Greece has the lowest proportion of population currently with access to the Internet. The average in the EU is some $8\frac{1}{2}$ per cent whilst Greece languishes with just 3 per cent. However, it is estimated that the current 300,000 subscribers will rise to around 800,000 within two years.

Public conveniences
Greek plumbing is notoriously bad. Your first culture shock is the realisation that toilet paper *etc* must be put into the waste bins and not down the toilet as this will cause a blockage. Public conveniences are not commonplace in Greece and you should get used to going into a *kafenío* and restaurants (*estiatório* or *tavérna*) and being prepared to ask for the use of their *toualéta*. Public toilets are located in a few parks and squares in the larger cities. If there is someone in attendance you should leave a small tip of about 100 GRD. Look out for the two doors *gynaikón* (ladies) and *andhrón* (gentlemen) — it's not always obvious which is which! Greek toilets are not renowned for being the most hygienic — don't always expect to find toilet paper.

Emptying the dustbins

There is a wealth of difference between the cities and the country. In the larger towns the refuse collection vans (*skorpédia*) will call on a regular basis usually weekly, whereas in more rural areas you may need to take your waste to a central collection point. Look out for the traditional method of waste disposal, tipping it down a mountain, which was fine in the days of purely bio-degradeable waste product.

Going shopping

The normal pattern for tourist areas is that shops open between 8.30 and 9.30 am and mostly close at lunchtime for the traditional siesta, opening again at about 5.00 pm and trading until 9.00 pm or so. The larger city shops, not dependent on tourism, follow UK times — largely speaking. Most government agencies are open to the public from 8 am to 2 pm, but by about 1 pm they tend to lose interest in fresh matters.

Large cash and carry supermarkets such as *Metro, Alpha Beta, Marinopolis* and *Sklabenitis* are familiar in Athens and in the larger cities now, although the smaller general stores are very much in evidence in villages *etc.* You will find mostly everything you need at these general stores. Be aware that pharmacies (*farmakío*) don't always open in the evenings or at weekends. However, they normally operate a rota system directing you via a sign on the door to the nearest point for obtaining drugs *etc.*

ORGANISING YOUR FINANCES

This can be relatively straightforward once you understand the best methods of organising yourself.

Paying the household bills

You should expect to receive three different bills:

- general utilities (heat, light, refuse collection *etc*) — four monthly (see Figure 6)
- telephone charges — two monthly (see Figure 8)
- water supply — three monthly (see Figure 9).

Utilities bills are calculated every four months but estimated bills are sent out every two. If you owe in excess of 2,500 GRD on a utilities bill you run the risk of having the service cut off. To get reconnected could cost 6-7,000 GRD, but you may be made to wait a considerable time.

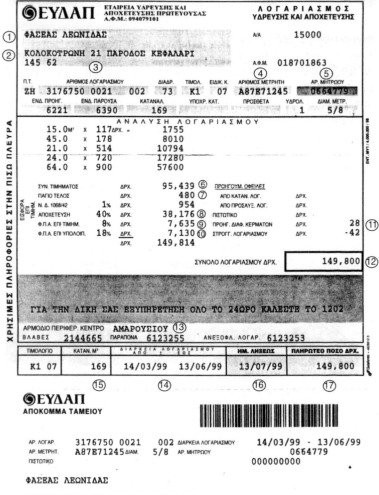

<0001498002+990613+06647798>

Key to Codes

1	Name	7	Fixed tax	13	Damages and breakdown
2	Address	8	Maintenance and drainage		telephone number
3	Account number	9	Local tax	14	Accounting period
4	Meter number	10	18% VAT	15	Consumption in units
5	Roll number	11	Rounding up/down	16	Date payable
6	Total price	12	Account total	17	Total amount payable

Fig. 9. Water bill.

Registering change of ownership
When you take over occupancy of a house *etc* you may be asked to visit the local police and present change of ownership documents to ensure that the utilities bills are raised in your name. In order to do this you will first need to purchase taxation stamps from a *períptero* and attach them to a simple statement in Greek explaining the change of occupancy. The police will then charge you extra to add their own particular stamps. The DEH (electricity company) will require an electrical report, which would normally be done with the topographical survey before transferring the property details into your name.

Working out the water bill
As water is clearly a scarce commodity, unless as a user you are a hotel, hospital etc you will be subjected to a contentious two tier pricing tariff. Quarterly bills for modest domestic use will be charged at a standard rate, but heavy users in excess of this sum will pay at a higher rate on the entire sum. In the rural areas water is paid for annually depending on consumption.

Considering a bank account

Greek banks (*trápeza*) normally open Monday to Thursday 8 am to 2 pm, Friday 8 am to 1.30 pm. Certain branches in the major cities and tourist centres are open extra hours in the evenings and on Saturday mornings for exchanging money. Always take your passport with you as proof of identity and be prepared for at least one long queue — you may have to line up once to have the transaction approved and again to pick up the cash.

Commissions vary depending on the bank and the size of the transaction — ask first. Both commission and rate will be worse if you change money at a hotel or travel agency.

You will need to consider whether to open an account in drachma or sterling and whether you want it to be with a state controlled bank, *eg* National Bank of Greece, or a private controlled bank, *eg* Agricultural Bank of Greece *etc*. Latterly, the state controlled banks do seem to be going on strike at regular intervals, although the charges and rates of interest are similar in both.

Opening a bank account
This is straightforward once you have produced proof of identity, your passport and 'pink slips' if appropriate showing how you have brought money into the country. In recent years the rate of inflation has gradually dropped from around 25 per cent to currently less than 3 per cent.

There is no uniformity on bank interest rates as each bank sets its own, but the state-owned National Bank of Greece, the biggest bank in Greece, is currently paying 6 to 7 per cent on drachma cash accounts and 5 to 6 per cent on UK sterling accounts depending on amount deposited. Interest is usually credited to your account twice a year, at which stage Greek tax will be deducted. It can be difficult to get an overdraft facility, which in any event may be very expensive. You should consider using the account to pay all of your household bills direct.

Pros and cons of Greek banks

Pros

- Security — your money is safe and locked away.

- A good drachma account can currently yield anywhere between about 6–8 per cent per annum, although Greek withholding tax of 15 per cent is deducted at source.

- A convenient way of having your household bills paid direct.

Cons

- Strikes — state owned banks in particular can close temporarily at a moment's notice. You never know when they may open again.

- Interpreting the bank statements unless you have a working knowledge of Greek.

- Opening hours can vary depending on seasons and days of the week.

KEEPING IN TOUCH

Nowadays with the advent of satellite TV in particular, European news is constantly available and up to date. However, there are other forms of communication that convey different kinds of news.

Reading newspapers

British newspapers are fairly widely available in Greece for 500–800 GRD, normally available at a *períptero* — albeit a day old on the islands and in the country but the same day in Athens. Local English language papers include the *Athens News*, which is good value at 300 GRD and available every day of the week except Mondays. The weekly *Hellenic Star* at 400 GRD is more in depth with wide coverage of what's on at cinemas, theatres, churches *etc*. The *Athens News* is now available on the Internet at *http://athensnews.dolnet.gr* enabling international readers and travellers to gain a fuller picture of the dailies' coverage.

Listening to the radio
Nearly all stations include music as a main feature. There are regular news bulletins and slots for tourist information in English on local Greek stations (try 412 medium wave at 7.30 am daily). The BBC World Service can be picked up on short wave frequencies throughout Greece on bandwidths normally between 15.15 – 19.00 MHz. The BBC in London publish a regular programming guide — see Useful Addresses.

Watching TV
Although with the advent of satellite and cable TV this form of media is changing, Greece has primarily two centralised government controlled TV stations, ET1 and ET3. Other available channels include NET, MEGA, ANTENNA, STAR and ALPHA showing everything from world sports, foreign soap operas and recent films from the cinema.

STARTING TO ENJOY LIFE

After the hassle of settling in, you will want to start exploring the area and find out things to do in your neck of the woods. Thanks to the fine climate, a lot of what's available can be enjoyed outdoors at a leisurely pace. There's nothing finer than sitting outside on a wonderful Greek evening watching the *volta*: locals parading past in their Sunday best.

Eating out
Now we come to the pleasant aspect of checking out where to go for good food and drink. Greek food is simple and straightforward. It needs to be as, unfortunately, Greece is not renowned for its cuisine. However, the Greeks do eat out a lot, possibly because of the climate, but also because they are such a wonderful sociable nation. You can choose to eat at many types of establishment.

Tavérna
The best strategy is to go where the Greeks go. Eat late, 2 pm to 3 pm for lunch, 9 pm to 11 pm for dinner. *Tavérnas* are the traditional eating

houses and will serve mostly baked, grilled or roast meat and fish. You will soon get used to the idea that Greeks do not bother about courses as such. All your food is likely to arrive at once, which is fine if you intend to share all the plates together. *Hors d'oeuvres* (*mezédhes*) can quite often be the best way of sampling what's on offer.

Look out for specialist *tavérnas*. *Psarotavérnes* will concentrate mainly on fish dishes whilst *psistariés* offer mostly spit roasted meats such as lamb, liver and goat.

Zaharoplastía

Most Greeks will eat their savoury food at a *tavérna*, then after having a brief walk around to aid digestion, they will settle at a *zaharoplastía* to partake of some coffee and sweetmeats, *eg baklavás* (honey and nut pastry), *galaktombóureko* (custard pie) and *kataífi* (shredded wheat covered in honey).

Galaktopolío

If your sweet tooth is more inclined towards dairy products then don't miss out on the excellent *rizógalo* (rice puddings), *kréma* (a custardy semolina), *yiaoúrti* (yoghurt) or *pagotó* (ice cream). These delicacies can be found at a *galaktopolió* where quite often all produce will be home made. Watch those calories though! Check out *pagotó me méli* (ice cream with honey) — the ultimate temptation.

Estiatório

Here you will normally find on offer a variety of oven baked casseroles. Choosing these dishes is commonly done by going to the kitchen and pointing at the desired trays. In many instances the food is cooked in the morning and then left to stand which is why it is quite often coldish. Greeks don't mind this as some of them believe that hot food is bad for you. Furthermore, certain dishes improve as they are left to marinate in their juices, but you will have to get used to receiving reheated chips, rice *etc*.

Kafenío

Traditionally a place where men gather to play cards or backgammon (*távli*), these are the street cafés or coffee shops popular for the lunchtime beer and toast/sandwich. You may sometimes find that they will serve you the time honoured (*horiátiki*) Greek salad — feta cheese, tomato, cucumber, olives in olive oil garnished with herbs. On a hot day the iced coffee (*kafés frappé*) can be really refreshing, especially with a scoop of ice-cream (*pagotó*) in it.

Sampling the nectar

The Greeks choose to drink to be sociable, whether lingering over a coffee or simply a carafe of wine at any time of the day or night.

Making the most of wine

Restaurants will usually offer you a choice of bottled wines and some may have their own house varieties kept in barrels and served out of metal jugs. The local house wine (*krasí dopio*) is always inexpensive and worth a try. Among the bottled wines Kambas, Boutari and Domestica are good inexpensive whites (*áspro*), whilst the reds (*mávro*) include Tsantali and Rotonda. Although not as fashionable as in years gone by, the pine resinated *retsína* has to be tried for the experience. You may care to try it mixed with Sprite or 7Up and ice as a long cool refreshing drink.

Drinking beer

The local Fix brewery in Athens has closed down leaving the field to Amstel, a lovely light but slightly perfumed Dutch lager bottled under licence in Greece, and the slightly more expensive Henniger (German lager) and the popular imports Heineken, Kronenberg and latterly Budweiser. You can still purchase a Greek brewed lager, Mythos, which is widely available. All these lagers are wonderfully refreshing at lunchtime as you sit and contemplate life, the universe and the wonder of it all.

Tasting the spirits

Basically there are two local drinks. *Oúzo* the aniseed based aperitif ideally drunk as the sun goes down with ice and a little water (*neró*), although there appears to be a popular tendency now for it to be mixed with lemonade. Occasionally, you can still come across the older established *ouzerí* where they will serve you *oúzo* and *mezédhes* together, a lovely way of trying all sorts of bits and pieces of fish, meat and vegetables on cocktail sticks. *Metaxá*, the local apricot brandy, is available as a three, five and seven star choice.

CASE STUDIES

Graham loses his mail

As Graham proposes to spend his time travelling the country and getting work where he can, it is difficult for him to let family and friends know of his whereabouts. However, he arranges via a friend in Athens to hold onto any mail which he will have sent on as soon as he finds semi-permanent accommodation. Whilst fine in theory, this idea doesn't really work as the post is taking so long from Athens to the islands that in some instances he has moved on to another job and location before the mail reaches him. After chatting about this predicament over an *oúzo* in a bar one night he is introduced to the excellent *poste restante* system, whereby friends and relatives can send mail on ahead to a main post office at the next nearest largish town he is likely to be travelling through. In this way, and at no further cost, all his mail is waiting for him.

Tony and Wendy are left dumbstruck

Tony and Wendy drive through Europe together with all their worldly possessions and savings to take up teaching posts in Athens. Unfortunately, no one informed them of the wisdom of declaring foreign exchange at the point of entering Greece and obtaining 'pink slips'. However, this is of no consequence until they register with the British Consul in Athens who advises them, that without proof of import of funds into Greece, they run the risk of being taxed on the foreign exchange when they attempt to deposit it into a bank account.

John and Betty get a telephone installed

Upon arriving at their old stone cottage on Skíathos, John immediately makes enquiries of the Greek telecommunications agency (OTE) about installing a telephone as quickly as possible. He is told that the good news is the cost would only be 38,000 GRD, but the bad news is no new lines are being installed in his village for at least 18 months. Being a determined type, and spurred on by Betty's constant requests to get her in contact more easily with their children and grandchildren, John sets off to the local *tavérna* to 'barter' for a line. Before long, he is introduced to Takis who runs a small fishing supplies business on the coastal road not far from John's house. After a few beers a deal is struck. For the princely sum of 75,000 GRD Takis will sell John one of his three lines provided John finds a local telecomms engineer to run the new line from Takis' shop to the cottage. This is done successfully and Betty immediately celebrates with a long distance, long duration call!

POINTS TO CONSIDER

1.   Tell the authorities that you have arrived in Greece. You never know when someone back home may need to contact you in an emergency. If you do move on, inform the nearest British consul of your

departure, intended destination, and then re-register as soon as you arrive.

2. Don't get cut off. Living on the islands is fine in the good weather, but come the storms the ferries will stop. Make sure you can get all the provisions and employment you are likely to need locally so that you are self-sufficient.

3. Think about having all your services bills paid directly via the bank. In this way you will avoid endless queues and no doubt arguments as everyone seems to push in just as it's your turn to be served.

6

Travelling Around

One of the great beauties of being in Greece is that there are many forms of transport for you to enjoy. Lawrence Durrell is quoted as saying in *Spirit of Place*, 'You should see the landscape of Greece. It would break your heart.'

DRIVING IN GREECE

Generally speaking, the further south in Europe you drive the more unpredictable the driving becomes — especially in Italy. However, Greek drivers, whilst not being the best in Europe, are certainly a lot better than some of their European counterparts. Nevertheless, Greece has the second highest accident rate in Europe after Portugal. You will encounter many variations of bad habits, including driving across the road to overtake on the wrong side, hooting at traffic signals when the lights are on red, and even driving through red traffic lights. Don't forget though, the horn is used to indicate the presence of another car, not necessarily that something's wrong.

Keep your eyes open as you drive along the mountain or coastal roads in particular, for the small roadside shrines which usually depict the scene of a fatal accident in the past. Sometimes the shrines are adorned by flowers or kept simple with a single light burning and a photograph.

Renting a car

Car rental in Greece is probably the most expensive in Europe. You should expect to pay a minimum of between 100,000 and 200,000 GRD per week for a fairly modest car for two adults and perhaps two children (see Figure 10). You can hire on the basis of either unlimited or fixed mileage. Extras will be added on such as insurance and tax. If you intend to enter a long term hire agreement, it may be better to consider hiring the car from the UK before your arrival. Most of the leading car hire

| | | LOW SEASON 01.04.2000-30.06.2000, 01.10.2000-31.03.2001 | | | | | HIGH SEASON 01.07.2000-30.09.2000 | | | | |
| | | Minimum charge 100 kms daily Ελάχιστη ημερήσια χρέωση 100 χλμ. | | Unlimited kilometer rates Χρέωση με ελεύθερα χλμ. | | | Minimum charge 100 kms daily Ελάχιστη ημερήσια χρέωση 100 χλμ. | | Unlimited kilometer rates Χρέωση με ελεύθερα χλμ. | | |
Group Κατηγορία	Type of car Τύπος αυτοκινήτου	Daily Ημερησίως	per Km ανά χλμ.	3 days 3 ημέρες	Weekly Εβδομαδιαίως	Add. day Επιπλέον ημέρα	Daily Ημερησίως	per Km ανά χλμ.	3 days 3 ημέρες	Weekly Εβδομαδιαίως	Add. day Επιπλέον ημέρα
	Manual										
A	FIAT SEICENTO DAEWOO MATIZ	5.400	90	65.600	107.500	15.400	6.600	113	81.500	133.700	19.100
B	SEAT IBIZA OPEL CORSA* FIAT PUNTO* CITROËN SAXO* NISSAN MICRA* HYUNDAI ATOS*	6.600	113	81.400	133.500	19.100	8.300	138	100.300	164.500	23.500
C	SEAT CORDOBA 1.4 A/C HYUNDAI ACCENT 1.3 A/C	9.200	148	108.900	178.700	25.500	11.300	165	125.800	206.500	29.500
D	TOYOTA COROLLA A/C OPEL ASTRA A/C FORD FOCUS A/C	11.800	161	124.500	203.500	29.100	14.800	174	142.700	233.200	33.300
E	MERCEDES A 140	12.000	164	127.000	207.600	29.700	15.100	177	145.600	237.900	34.000
F	OPEL VECTRA 1.6 A/C TOYOTA AVENSIS 1.6 A/C SEAT TOLEDO 1.6 A/C	16.100	178	154.600	255.500	36.500	19.800	227	194.300	321.300	45.900
G	BMW 316 A/C	24.500	245	N/A	N/A	N/A	31.200	313	N/A	N/A	N/A
	Luxury										
H	MERCEDES C 180 A/C	36.000	361	N/A	N/A	N/A	42.700	426	N/A	N/A	N/A
I	SAAB 9-5 A/C MERCEDES E 200 A/C	40.600	405	N/A	N/A	N/A	46.600	466	N/A	N/A	N/A
	Automatic										
J	SEAT AROSA A/C	12.600	120	111.400	184.200	26.300	14.200	166	140.800	232.800	33.300
K	TOYOTA COROLLA 1.3 A/C HYUNDAI ACCENT 1.3 A/C	13.200	144	125.900	208.200	29.700	16.100	186	158.400	261.900	37.400
L	OPEL VECTRA 1.6 A/C	21.800	218	193.400	317.200	45.300	26.300	293	248.000	406.800	58.100
M	SAAB 9-5 A/C	42.600	426	N/A	N/A	N/A	50.700	507	N/A	N/A	N/A
	Minibus										
X	NISSAN SERENA 1.6 A/C**	19.800	235	196.500	323.800	46.300	26.200	277	243.000	400.500	57.200
Y	FIAT SCUDO 1.8 A/C*** FORD TOURNEO 2.0 A/C***	23.700	266	224.400	368.000	52.600	32.900	332	293.400	481.300	68.800

Special Vehicles

Station Wagon: SEAT CORDOBA VARIO 1.4 A/C **Open - 4x4:** CHRYSLER CHEROKEE, SSANGYONG MUSSO, SUZUKI VITARA **Open Top:** SAAB 900 TURBO A/C CABRIO, PEUGEOT 306 CABRIO, RENAULT TWINGO, FIAT PUNTO CABRIO **Multipurpose:** SEAT ALHAMBRA ESCAPE 2.0 A/C, FIAT MULTIPLA, CITROËN PICASSO, OPEL ZAFIRA

For more information see SPECIAL VEHICLES TARIFF

Όλα τα αυτοκίνητα διαθέτουν ραδιοκασετόφωνο. A/C: Air condition N/A: Δεν διατίθενται ** 7-8 seats * Διατίθενται με κλιματισμό με πρόσθετη χρέωση δρχ. 2.500 ημερησίως.
All cars are fitted with Radio-cassette. S/W: Station Wagon N/A: Not Available *** 9 seats Available with air-conditioning at an extra charge.

Fig. 10. Car hire tariff card.

79

agencies have representatives in Athens (details in Useful Addresses). If you have an accident it is likely that the car hire agency will not collect or lend you another vehicle. You may have to wait for two or three days for a representative to visit and assess the situation.

Signing the papers
All car hire agencies will demand either a credit card or substantial cash deposit in advance. The minimum age to hire ranges from 21 to 25. You should also produce an international driver's licence and ensure that the car has breakdown insurance with the Greek Automobile Association (ELPA). Some car rental companies have an agreement with ELPA's competitors, Hellas Service and Express Service, but they are prohibitively expensive to call out. The cost can be over 45,000 GRD to enrol you on the spot.

Reading the small print
Be wary, in many cases initial rental prices quoted may not include taxation, collision damage waiver fees and personal insurance. The coverage included by Greek law in the basic rental fee is generally inadequate. *Caveat emptor* — let the buyer beware, check the fine print on your contract.

Buying a car

In many of the larger cities, Athens, Thessaloniki, Pátras *etc*, second hand Greek cars can be bought from garages. Be cautious, maintenance of these vehicles will not necessarily be what we have been used to in the UK. A good source for buying a car in Greece is the English language newspapers, such as the *Athens News* and the *Hellenic Star*. Contract workers looking to return to the UK will normally pass on a well maintained vehicle to you. Once again, if you know you are going to be in Greece for a period of time it is usually better to purchase a sturdy diesel vehicle in the UK and drive it the 1,500 miles or so through Europe to Greece with twelve months UK MOT and some Greek insurance to get you going. Refer to Chapter 2 for the legislation.

Keeping legal

Greek vehicle insurance is available through most of the large European insurance companies based in Athens, *eg* General Accident. You should always display the policy in its plastic folder on your windscreen. A good source of information is the British Hellenic Chamber of Commerce which publishes an annual directory of members including motor insurance companies with UK representatives in Athens. You do not require

Greek road tax for the first six months your car is in Greece, thereafter it is calculated according to the size of your engine. It starts from 25,000 GRD per annum for vehicles up to 1400cc, then increases to 45,000 GRD per annum for vehicles to 1600c and thereafter 65,000 GRD per annum. However, this amount can be reduced upon production of sufficient 'pink slips' to show you have imported substantial foreign exchange into Greece.

Greeks are required by law to MOT their car once a year but this appears to be policed very little. However, smoke emission is taken somewhat more seriously. The requirement is for a test every two years. Provided that the vehicle complies, a small circular sticker is put on the number plate at the rear of the car to show it has been tested and when it is valid until.

If you are unfortunate enough to be involved in a minor incident, you do not need to report the accident to the police unless someone is injured. If this is the case, get witnesses, preferably English speaking, who are prepared to testify to what they saw.

A word of warning, EU nationals (including Greeks) cannot drive diesel cars in the wider regions of Athens and Thessaloníki. There is no problem in the rest of Greece.

Checking out the fuel

Petrol currently costs slightly less per litre than in the UK — about 275 GRD for leaded and 260 GRD for unleaded. Diesel is substantially cheaper in Greece — about 225 GRD, and this should be a consideration if you are looking to bring in a car. The 24 hour service station is only occasionally seen in certain parts of the larger cities such as Athens. Most garages tend to shut at about 7 pm: some of them may shut all weekend. Local knowledge goes a long way, and there should always be at least one pump locally open at the weekend. Unlike the pharmacies, no rota list is posted, so trust to luck and you should run across the single station. If in doubt, the local tourist police (*touristikí astinomiá*) should be able to advise. Normally, you will find a station open close to the major national roads.

If you are new to an area, and are hiring a car, then try and ensure that you pick it up with a full tank of fuel. If you are likely to be driving in remote areas then it is advisable to keep a full five litre petrol can in the boot, although strictly speaking this is illegal.

Keeping documents in the car

Should you be stopped while driving in Greece, which is always likely as long as you are driving a right hand drive vehicle, there is a chance you may be asked to produce the following documents:

- car hire rental contract
- details of your accommodation
- European driving licence
- lease hire contract (if appropriate)
- passport
- permission to drive vehicle if not your own
- proof of when the vehicle was imported to Greece (original ferry tickets *etc*)
- vehicle registration V5.

Whilst the list may seem comprehensive, it is always advisable to have all these documents to hand. Ensure you have the original form V5 Vehicle Registration available if the car is yours — not a photocopy. With car theft on the increase, however, it is advisable to keep photo-copies only of all other documents in the car.

Changing over to Greek plates

To avoid the formal process of either removing your vehicle from the country for six months every 15 months, or having it locked up by Customs officials and therefore unusable for this period (see Chapter 2) you could consider registering the vehicle for Greek plates. You will be asked to pay a one-off registration fee based on the perceived value of the car followed by an annual road tax based on engine cc and, in the case of Greek residents, level of earnings.

TAKING IT EASY

By far the cheapest form of public transport for getting around in Greece is the train, but there are more buses travelling around Greece than any other public vehicle. For the romantic traveller there are some lovely train routes to follow, but unfortunately the network can be slow and limited. The best way to supplement buses and trains is to rent a car, motorbike or moped, especially on islands or in larger towns where you should find a rental agency. Moving between the islands calls for ferries, which are extensive but do not necessarily run on time or run at all depending on the weather. Domestic air flights are the most expensive form of transport but clearly the quickest.

Using the railway

The Greek railway network is operated by OSE which quite often is limited to the mainland and can be a slow service. The exception is the excellent Athens to Peloponnese service which travels over the Corinth canal from Athens and then either takes the coastal road via Pátras to Kalamáta or goes straight over the mountains via Trípolis to Kalamáta. Timetables are sporadic at the best of times, mostly printed in Greek and available from OSE offices in the larger towns. It is always advisable to check the station notices as this will give you up to date news. Timetables may only be printed annually and can quickly become out of date. You should always be on time for a train but be mindful that they can be up to 45 minutes late in leaving.

If you are planning a long journey, it is worthwhile booking a seat. This costs very little more and avoids the inevitable push and shove as everyone clambers on for available seats. You will be allocated a carriage and seat number which you will find on the back of your ticket. Note that the number shown on your ticket should correspond to the seat you actually sit on and not the number plate on the back of the seat in front of you.

Deciding on the right class of travel
Normally there are two types of rail travel, standard or second class and first class. First class is always worth the additional money as you will find the carriages larger, less crowded and certainly more comfortable. Recently a luxury sleeper category (*tréna/ksenodhohiá*) has been introduced to the more popular routes between Pátras, Athens, Thessaloniki, Vólos and Alexandria. These trains travel overnight at high speed, but once again don't always trust the timetable.

Saving on tickets
Inter-rail passes and Euro-train tickets are available through local tour operators, but as a competitor, OSE also sells its own pass which can offer unlimited travel for ten, 20 and 30 days.

Riding the metro

Athens has a well established single metro/underground line which stretches from Piraeus in the south to the lovely garden suburb of Kifissia some 14 kms north east of Athens centre. A long overdue extension and modernisation programme for the underground system is due to be completed in 2001 (see Figure 11). The first two lines have been functioning since January 2000, connecting with the existing system. The project has

It is the largest and most complex transportation construction project currently in Greece and one of the largest in Europe. The new underground Metro system consists of two lines radiating in four directions from Syntagma Square to Pentagono, Dafni, Sepolia and Keramikos.

A total of 21 stations will be built, serving approximately 450,000 daily passengers when the system becomes operational in 2001. This is in addition to the 300,000 passengers currently being served by the existing Metro line connecting Pireas with Omonia Square and Kifissia. For fast and efficient service, trains will run every 3 minutes in rush hour, and every 5-10 minutes in non-rush hour. The two new lines will connect with the existing Metro line at Omonia, Monastiraki and Attiki Stations.

Plans to extend the system to serve the outer districts of Athens are underway.

Fig. 11. The new Athens metro.

understandably been delayed not only by the inevitable bureaucracy, but also by the many archaeological finds along the way. These include ancient roads, a bath house, aqueducts, remnants of the original city walls, and two shops, one selling marble and the other vases from the fourth and fifth century BC — vases which, when lit up, appear most revealing in a pornographic sense! Look out for the archaeological remains found whilst excavating on display at the new Metro station at Syntagma Square. At 250 GRD to ride its entire length, the Athens metro is amongst the cheapest in Europe, although it can work out even cheaper if you buy a 'go anywhere' ticket for 1,000 GRD per day or 10,000 GRD per month. A scheme is currently being planned to introduce an underground system in Thessaloniki.

Travelling by bus and coach

As there are more buses than any other form of public transport, you would expect them to be highly efficient, and regular. This may well be so on the important routes, but on the secondary roads they can be less regular with long halts for coffee, *souvláki etc*. Even the most remote villages will be connected, if only with one bus a day. You will find that buses to the outlying regions leave the major centres shortly after dawn. On the islands, there are always buses to connect the port and main town ferry arrivals and departures.

Unlike the trains, buses are amazingly prompt, so be there in plenty of time for scheduled departures. For the major inter-city lines such as Athens to Pátras, you will find that ticketing is computerised and automatically allocates seats. Back to basics on the islands, it is generally 'first come first served' with quite a lot of standing space allowed for you, your mother and your pets! You will be able to buy tickets either from the driver or quite often at a local *kafenío*. A few long distance and international routes are also served by express buses operated by OSE, the state railway organisation.

Coaching it

Most of the coach network consists of green and cream coloured buses privately run by a syndicate of companies known as the KTEL. However, even in medium sized towns there can be several scattered terminals for services in different directions, so make sure you have the right station for your departure.

Cruising on the ferries

Greece has a number of major sea ports including Piraeus, Pátras, Vólos,

Thessaloniki, Heraklion and Igoumenitsa. You can expect to find three different types of boats: medium sized to large ordinary ferries which operate the main services, hydro-foils, such as the Flying Dolphins, and thirdly *kaikía*, which are the small boats which in season cover the short island hops and excursions. Costs are normally reasonable on the longer journeys although disproportionately more expensive for the shorter inter-island connections. Out of season, departure frequencies are severely reduced with many islands connected only once or twice a week.

The most reliable and up to date information is available from the local port police (*limenarhíó*). Unfortunately they don't always speak English but you will find timetables posted. For those with a sensitive constitution, weather reports are normally listed and if a storm is brewing be prepared for the crossing to be cancelled.

Flying across Greece

Greece has 36 commercial airports, of which 23 are international, albeit some seasonal. The main airports are at Athens, Thessaloniki, Crete, Rhodes and Corfu. All domestic flights are operated by Olympic Airways, its subsidiary Olympic Aviation and a few new operators including Aegean. A fairly wide network of islands and larger towns is covered, although most routes begin and end at Athens or the northern capital of Thessaloniki. Both main airlines are in the process of being privatised and as fares continue to rise annually you should be aware that this is by far the most expensive way to travel. Timetables are available from the Olympic offices in Syntagma Square, Athens.

Buying tickets

Fares usually work out at about three or four times the cost of an equivalent bus or ferry journey. Island flights are often full in mid-season, therefore as in the UK purchase your tickets at least three or four days in advance to be sure. Note that the domestic air tickets are non-refundable, but you can change flight details without incurring further costs. As with the ferries, flights can be cancelled in bad weather largely because the inter-island hoppers tend to be small turbo prop planes that will carry between 15 and 30 people. Due to the size of these small airplanes, your 20 kilo international allowance will be brought down to about 15 kilos. Don't expect in-flight films or *oúzo*!

Catching taxis

Especially in Athens, the taxi is invaluable and can be a very reasonable way of getting around, although devilishly difficult to find when you want one. You are unlikely to find an empty taxi in Athens. Always hail a taxi that uses the meter system. You should start your journey at 200 GRD and will be asked to pay a surcharge for such extras as:

- 50 GRD for each piece of baggage put in the boot
- 200 GRD for being driven to a ferry port
- 300 GRD for being driven to an airport.

You will be expected to pay double the clock rates between 1 am and 5 am. If you go outside the city or town limits you will also find yourself on double time. Come Christmas and Easter, prices may go up legitimately by about a third more than displayed.

Watching out for pirates
Once you are outside the larger cities, the small businessman comes into his own and taxis may have no meters. Watch out for pirates, especially from the airports. There are also many of them around the train stations and bus depots. If they are not licensed, you could be charged any figure they have in mind. If your Greek is not too good, you lay yourself open to extortion. However, allow about 200 GRD per kilometre per average journey. Beware the taxi driver who already has one or more passengers when he picks you up: you will be expected to pay the normal full rate for your journey, but you should note the fare on the meter when he picks you up, and deduct it from the final destination tariff before offering cash. Don't forget, though, to add 200 GRD to the final sum for the 'standing charge'. As these drivers are operating illegally, you cannot be sure how well the vehicle is maintained.

Hitchhiking around
Undoubtedly one of the loveliest ways of getting around Greece is on your thumb. The Greeks are very good about giving lifts. Generally speaking, vans and lorries will stop for you, but, increasingly, commercial vehicles are not allowed to offer rides.

Pros and cons of hitchhiking

Pros

- Cheap — it costs you nothing.
- Exciting — you get to meet people from all walks of life.
- Adventurous — it brings out the spirit of travel.

Cons

- Can be dangerous, especially for single women on their own and at night.
- Frustrating — you don't always end up where you had planned or anticipated.
- Time consuming — it can take hours to get a lift.

Making the most of motorbikes

Mopeds are perfect for all but the hilliest areas and are available everywhere as a tourist attraction. Make sure you look them over thoroughly, as sometimes unscrupulous operators will ensure that they are clean but not necessarily safe. Normally if you break down it is your responsibility to return the machine, so it is worth noting the telephone number of the agency in case you get stranded. It is not fashionable in Greece to wear a crash helmet but you should put your safety first. Wear long trousers to ensure that you do not burn your legs on the exhaust pipe.

If you are likely to be in Greece for some time it is well worth considering the purchase of a moped or motorbike as they are inexpensive to run and can be moved to and from the islands on a ferry, and also re-sold very easily upon departure. You would not normally expect to be stopped by the police when you are on two wheels.

Cycling is fun

A mountain bike is a great idea in Greece, especially portable ones that can be packed on trains and aeroplanes. The beauty of this is that you can mostly take bicycles free of charge on ferries and in the guard's van on trains. Most Greek buses tend to have roof racks and will gladly carry your bicycle provided they are not already over-burdened with luggage. As with motorbikes, always wear a hard hat.

KEEPING ON THE RIGHT SIDE OF THE LAW

It's one thing to understand the Greek law, but quite another to abide by it, try as you might.

Understanding the rules of the road

International road signs are in use throughout Greece. You drive on the right, pass on the left and allow right of way to all vehicles approaching from the right, except on main roads. Watch out on the roundabouts. At a busy time of day, mayhem will ensue. Stick to your guns and don't be harassed.

Keeping within the speed limits

The speed limits tend to be 30-50 KPH in built up areas, 100 KPH on all other roads unless lower limits are displayed. Often, however, no speed limits are shown and even when they are many Greeks don't obey them.

Parking in town

In many of the larger towns you will find underground and on-street meter car parks. In many cities, parking on just one side of the street is permitted to facilitate traffic passing. Parking on the pavement is common, but lately the police appear to be clamping down on this illegal practice.

Checking the vehicle's contents

Recently the police have become considerably stricter with cars on the road, regularly inspecting at random to ensure each vehicle contains:

● fire extinguisher
● first aid kit
● spare lamp bulbs
● vehicle documents
● warning triangle.

You can also expect the odd alcohol test. The police have powers to impose on-the-spot fines if they are not happy with the vehicle for whatever reason. Use of seat belts is compulsory, although most Greeks do not wear seat belts themselves. No child under the age of ten may travel in the front.

Breaking down

By law you must put out a red triangle danger sign if you break down. The Greek national breakdown service ELPA is always close to hand on the major roads. Unlike many other European countries, the service is free but a tip is expected, provided you have proof of AA/RAC membership. ELPA has breakdown centres in Athens, Ioannína, Corfu, Crete, Lárissa, Pátras, Trípolis and Vólos. While in Greece, dial 174 for information and 104 in an emergency.

Travelling the motorways

The national road network stretches for about 40,000 kilometres, of which nearly 9,000 are national roads. The few motorways in Greece link Athens, Pátras, Thessaloníki and Vólos. Road tolls are cheap, normally about 500–900 GRD per section. (See Figure 4.) Not all toll booths will be manned. Quite often there will be a large net outside the toll point and you will be expected to drop the exact change into it.

Policing the area

Greece has three types of police force (*astinomiá*). The tourist police (*touristikí astinomiá*) usually wear uniforms with flags on their jackets identifying the languages they speak. As well as helping visitors generally, they also act as state inspectors of hotels and restaurants to ensure that proper standards and prices are maintained. Local police operating outside the city boundaries are called *chorofílakes*. They wear shoulder cordons with their green uniforms and are seen in white helmets on motorcycles. Finally, Athens has a separate municipal police force, *astinomiá póleon*. The officers drive white patrol cars and wear dark blue uniforms.

POINTS WORTH KNOWING

Along the way, you will soon discover various tips and techniques to ease your way through the transportation system.

Registering an accident

If you are involved in an accident where someone is injured, it is illegal to drive away without registering the incident with the police. Failure to do so can result in being held in a police station for up to 24 hours. If you feel that you are not being understood or the accident is serious ring the British consul immediately in order to get a lawyer. Don't make a statement to anyone who doesn't speak and write very good English; certainly don't sign any paper, official or otherwise, without fully understanding what has been written.

Being aware of the environment

To ease pollution in Athens city centre, the government has from time to time introduced restrictions that apply to local cars, including hired vehicles. Currently these restrictions include that private vehicles with odd number plates can circulate in the town centre on odd numbered days of the month and even numbered plates on even numbered dates. However, the authorities now turn a blind eye to offenders as they swiftly came to the conclusion that they lacked the manpower to police the volume of traffic. The restrictions apply on weekdays until 8 pm. Also, to ease pollution, a small triangle of roads close to Syntagma Square in Athens has been designated pedestrians only. This has got the taxi drivers up in arms. Other schemes such as covering the Parthenon in a glass bubble, and driving the opposite way around the Acropolis, have been considered over the years to help prevent further decay to the ancient monument.

The Mayor of Athens has recently turned his attention to litterbugs. Apparently there is now an instant fine of 3,000 GRD for anyone caught dropping litter from a car window. Bulk items left on the pavement without authorisation will elicit a fine of up to 50,000 GRD.

Changing your driving licence

The holder of a driving licence from the UK may exchange it for a Greek licence without taking a driving test. The *quid pro quo* is that this application must be made within one year of taking up residence. The previous licence must be surrendered to the licensing authorities. A Greek driving licence remains valid until the holder reaches the age of 65 after which an application for extension is required.

Losing your car

Car theft is common in the larger towns, not so in the smaller villages where everyone is to be trusted and leaves their vehicle unlocked when unattended. Make sure you have copies of any original documents you propose to leave in the car. The Greek insurance claims process can be slow and arduous. Always report a theft immediately to the police and get an incident report or number for your insurance company.

CASE STUDIES

Graham wastes time

After staying a few days in Athens at the YMCA soaking up the culture, Graham decides to head north to the industrial town of Thessaloniki. Catching a bus to the city limits, he starts hitching a lift alongside the Athens-Lárissa national road. Before long, a dilapidated old truck carrying fruit pulls up and Graham shows the driver his placard with his destination written on it. With a huge toothless grin, the driver beckons Graham into the cab and they set forth, accompanied by loud *bouzoúki* music on the radio, and wildly swaying giant worry beads (*kombolói*) hanging from the interior mirror. After nearly three hours the driver pulls over at a roadside *kafenió* for refreshment. One thing leads to another, a coffee and cigarette then another coffee, someone gets out the backgammon set (*távli*) and Graham realises he has been sitting waiting for nearly two hours. As dusk is fast approaching and accommodation needs to be found, Graham decides to thank the driver and move on. Within minutes, a car stops and Graham is whisked off down the road at speed. Unfortunately, when the car pulls off the national road the driver insists on taking Graham to meet his family some 50 km distant. Graham is not pleased, but you can't refuse Greek hospitality.

Tony and Wendy get stopped

Mindful of the legislation about documents and safety items to be kept in the car at all times, Tony and Wendy are careful, every time they drive in Athens, to take their documents folder with them. They have heard of the random spot checks by the Greek police, especially of right hand drive vehicles. Sure enough, one evening after visiting the lovely open air cinema out of town at Kifissia, they are stopped in a cordial manner and asked to produce their documents which they duly do — but then to their consternation they are asked to produce passports, which they can't. The police motorcyclist, obviously keen to do things properly, insists that Tony report to the nearest police station the following day with both passports. Startled at having to carry passports everywhere within an EU member country, Tony and Wendy return home.

John and Betty travel first class

John and Betty decide, after spending a few days decorating their old cottage on Skíathos, to visit the neighbouring islands of Skópelos, Alónissos and Skíros. They choose to travel by the Russian manufactured 'Flying Dolphin' hydrofoils which run a regular inter-island service. However, despite buying tickets well in advance as advised, they find themselves without a seat on the return Alónissos-Skíathos leg of the journey. They complain to a stewardess, who is extremely sympathetic and moves them into the tiny first class section without further cost. John and Betty feel like royalty as they are transported in exclusive comfort back to their dream cottage.

POINTS TO CONSIDER

1. Think about what would happen if you lost your passport, travellers cheques, currency and other important documents whilst travelling around. Have you kept duplicates? Have you adequate insurance on the cash and cheques? Do you know who to call for help? — (details of British consuls in Useful Addresses).

2. Plan your travel arrangements carefully. Avoid the hassle of pushing and shoving trying to get onto public transport. Buy your tickets well in advance.

3. Invest in a good set of maps. The bookshops in Athens mentioned in Useful Addresses can help. Up to recently only military maps showed detail, but these were not commercially available due to the potential threat of the Turkish taking advantage. However, the decision of the European Council meeting in Helsinki during December 1999 to make Turkey the thirteenth candidate for enlargement of the EU should go a long way to easing tensions and improving relations between the two countries, which have traditionally patrolled borders in anticipation of hostile action.

7

Health and Welfare

Greece demonstrates its many charms as a country of converging cultures, where east meets west, not least in the way the support services are administered.

UNDERSTANDING THE HEALTH SYSTEM

The Greek national health system is run by IKA, otherwise known as *idrima kinonikon asfalisseon*. The Greeks tend to look after themselves in many respects although, generally, employees, the self employed and their dependants are entitled to free social security health assistance. However, 'free' means admittance only to the lowest grade of state hospital (*yenikó nosokomío*) and does not include nursing care or the cost of medication. If you need long term medical care, you would be better off seeking private treatment, which is very expensive, although many organisations provide comprehensive health plans with international insurance agencies. There is an efficient network of hospitals and clinics in the Athens area.

Dealing with emergencies

Assuming you can get near a telephone in a hurry, the vital numbers you will need are:

- ambulance   166
- emergency doctor   105
- fire service   199
- local police   100
- tourist police   171

These calls are free. The municipal hospital at *Leoforós Mesogíon* in Athens has a 24 hour emergency clinic three days a week. If you telephone on any other day they will direct you to the nearest clinic in operation.

Treating minor injuries

Treatment is given free in state hospitals for cuts and abrasions, broken bones *etc*, although you will only get the most basic level of nursing care. Greek families are expected to take in food and provisions for relatives. A better class of care can be found at the state run out-patient clinics (*yatría*) found linked to most state hospitals. These operate on a 'first come, first served' basis, usually from 8 am to noon, and will treat all kinds of injuries.

Getting health services when unemployed

If you are unemployed and looking for work then you should carry a form E111 which will enable you to receive urgent medical treatment free in Greece should you need it. The form E111 is available from any UK Post Office or Department of Social Security office. In addition, if you are not paying Greek national insurance contributions or covered by the form E111, it is advisable to take out private medical insurance or you may face the possibility of paying the full price for any treatment.

Continuing unemployment from the UK

Anyone coming to look for work in Greece who was unemployed in the UK, is entitled to free medical treatment in Greece if they produce form E119 at the local IKA office. This is also issued by the local Department of Health Office in the UK. In both the above cases IKA will exchange the form for a medical booklet.

Claiming medical expenses when back in the UK

If you are in Greece for only a short period and do not make a claim for medical expenses incurred while you are there, then retain all your medical bills, receipts and other documentation and return these with your E111 to the overseas branch of the Department of Social Services (see Useful Addresses) on your return.

Pros and cons of the state system

Pros:

● Free — it costs you nothing.

● Wide range of hospitals, doctors and dentists available.

● Unlimited period of stay in hospital.

Cons

- Level of nursing — your family is expected to nurse you and sometimes provide blankets.

- Long waits to get attention.

- Not always a guarantee of getting an English speaking doctor. Most hospital staff, including nurses, will not be able to speak English at all.

WORKING IN THE SYSTEM

It is important that you recognise the differences between being a tourist and working for a living during your stay.

Starting work

When you start work you must obtain a medical booklet (*iatrico vivliario*) from the local IKA office which you must take with you on all visits to the doctor or hospital. Your local IKA office can provide a list of doctors who work within the recognised national health system. The European Community has published a booklet, *Social Security for Migrant Workers*, which is available from the Overseas Branch of the DSS (see Useful Addresses).

Getting injured at work

If you are unlucky enough to have an accident at work, you should notify the local IKA office within five days. You can get information on your health rights by contacting the overseas branch of the Department of Social Services. If you are in Greece then contact the IKA office or the International Relations Office (*Tmima Diethon Scheseon*). The Department of Health in the UK has produced a leaflet entitled *Health Advice for Travellers within the EC*, which is available from most UK Post Offices. Any employee injured as a result of their employment is entitled to compensation and/or a disability pension for the period of absence from work, irrespective of the period previously employed. The amount paid by IKA is the same as for sickness benefit.

Finding out about other allowances

It's always worth checking at your local IKA office as financial allowances are made for marriage, holding a degree from a recognised educational institution, unhealthy or dangerous work and for seniority.

LIVING IN THE PRIVATE SECTOR

Greece has over 550 hospitals. However, you may find that you do not have adequate medical facilities nearby, particularly if you choose to live out of town. Private health insurance is recommended. Before buying, check out local facilities and how quickly you can reach a major hospital in an emergency. Long waits for treatment in both local offices, surgeries and hospitals are standard. If you decide to approach Greek doctors and hospitals direct for private treatment, then the state arrangements will not apply and you will be responsible for the full cost of any treatment received. You should therefore take out sufficient private insurance to cover full costs for yourself and your family, preferably before you leave the UK.

Paying for medical treatment

Doctor and hospital treatment within the Greek national health system as stated is free. However, you will be charged 25 per cent of the cost of any prescribed medication. If you live in a remote area of Greece which is not covered by a local IKA office, then you will have to pay the cost of any private medical treatment yourself, and make a retrospective claim for the cost from the IKA office in Athens. Unfortunately, the refund will only be a proportion of the cost and you will be liable for the balance. If you do receive treatment under these circumstances, you must obtain receipts and documentation to submit with your claim.

Considering your well-being

To put your mind completely at ease, take out health insurance to cover the risk of illness and accident whilst in Greece. Your travel agent or insurance company in the UK will be able to advise you. Although there are no mandatory inoculations required for Greece, it is always sensible to have the typhoid-cholera booster and to check that you are up to date on polio and tetanus.

UNDERSTANDING THE WELFARE SYSTEM

IKA administers the health, sickness, maternity and old age benefits. OAED (*Organisimos Apasholisseos Ergatikou Dynamikou*) handles issues relating to family and unemployment benefits. Social security contributions are deducted at source by employers and paid direct to IKA. The employer pays the social security on behalf of the employee. The total amount of social security contributions is payable monthly by the employer. Penalties for late payment to the social security funds are imposed subject to a maximum of 120 per cent. In addition, there is a penalty of 50 per cent for failing to register the employee. This is increased to 75 per cent if the employee is non-resident or receives a pension. The contributions are based on the employee's monthly salary which, including the statutory bonuses, is payable 14 times per annum. The maximum monthly salary on which contributions are payable is revised every four months in accordance with the automatic inflation adjustment applicable to minimum wage levels – see Figure 12.

Table of social security contributions

Fund	Employer	Employee	Total
IKA	24.96%	12.90%	37.86%
TEAM	3.00%	3.00%	6.00%
Total	27.96%	15.90%	43.86%

You should note that these contributions are increased in certain rural areas or where the work is hazardous or of a heavy nature.

Fig. 12. Social security contributions.

Learning the differences

Interestingly enough, Greece does not at present have a uniform social security system. There are many different social security agencies covering various sectors of the population. For example, there are separate entities for the legal profession, teachers, engineers, shopkeepers, farmers and employed persons in general. All funds are under the direction of the Ministry of Social Services. In addition to the basic social security funds, employed persons must also be covered by a supplementary retirement fund. The main funds available to employed persons are the social retirement fund (IKA) and the employees' supplementary retirement fund (TEAM).

Being unemployed

Employees are entitled to unemployment compensation for a period of five to twelve months depending on the period for which they were previously employed and during which they contributed to the social security funds. The maximum unemployment compensation varies, depending on the maximum salary on which social security contributions are payable and the number of dependant family members of the insured employee.

Transferring Job Seeker's Allowance (JSA)

If you are entitled to the contributions part of JSA which you have been claiming in the UK for at least four weeks before your departure, you may continue to receive the allowance for up to a further 12 weeks in Greece whilst job-hunting. You should inform your UK Job Centre of your intentions well before departure date. Your local Job Centre will inform the DSS Overseas Branch, which will decide whether you will be entitled to claim JSA in Greece, and if so, send to your UK address form E303 which you must present to the nearest Job Centre in Greece upon arrival. Further information on this matter can be found at any UK Job Centre in a brochure (JSAL 22) and also deatailed leaflet SA29 *Your Social Security, Insurance, Benefits and Health Care Rights in the European Community and in Norway, Iceland and Liechenstein.* See Useful Addresses.

Getting sickness benefit

Persons insured by IKA for at least 140 working days are entitled to medical treatment by IKA doctors free of charge and dental treatment at a reduced cost. Medicines prescribed by doctors may generally be obtained free of charge. In addition to the above an insured employee is entitled to collect sickness benefit. The maximum sickness benefit paid by IKA is adjusted regularly, based on a maximum remuneration on which social security is payable. In case of sickness, the employer is obliged to pay up to one month's salary to each employee. However, the amount payable by the employer is reduced by the relevant amount paid out by the social insurance fund.

Transferring UK sickness benefit

If you are in receipt of sickness benefit in the UK you may be able to transfer payment to Greece. Ask at your local Department of Social Services office in the UK for further information. The Benefits Agency web site is *www.dss.gov.uk/ba*. Claims for sickness benefit are made on your behalf by your employer to the local IKA office. Further information is also given in leaflet SA29 (see above).

Understanding maternity benefits

Employers may not terminate the employment of pregnant women. A lump sum benefit is payable upon the birth of a child but the benefit is paid to the husband when the mother is not insured. In addition, the insured mother is entitled to maternity leave of 16 weeks; 56 days preceding the expected date of delivery and 56 days following, in respect of which a benefit is receivable determined in the same manner as for the sickness benefit. Employers may not terminate the employment of a woman until her child reaches 1 year of age.

Registering as a pensioner

Pensions payable are dependent on the period over which contributions were paid, the age of the individual and the salary in the two years preceding retirement. An employee is entitled to a full pension after making contributions relating to just over 10,000 working days, completing 35 years of employment and reaching at least 58 years of age. Reduced pensions are payable: in order to qualify, an individual is generally required to have made contributions in respect of about 4,500 working days. A retirement pension is usually paid at the age of 65 and over for men and 60 for women.

Under EEA regulations, if you work in two or more EU countries you can consolidate state pension contributions paid in each country in order to qualify for a state pension. Once again, before leaving the UK you are advised to discuss this with the Overseas Branch of the DSS (see Useful Addresses). Alternatively, visit any IKA office whilst in Greece.

Pensioners who intend to take up residence in Greece and who are entitled to free medical treatment in the UK enjoy a similar entitlement in Greece. They should produce at their local IKA office form E121, which is issued by their local Department of Health office in the United Kingdom.

Claiming child allowance

A tax credit of 30,000 GRD per child is given provided they are under the age of 18, or under the age of 22 in the case of students living in Greece, unless the employee is subject to a collective labour agreement which provides for the payment of the child allowance by the employer.

CONSIDERING OTHER MATTERS

The nuances of the Greek system take a little getting used to. The following observations should help.

Dealing with foreign employees

Foreign employees may in certain circumstances, *eg* temporary employment, be exempt from registering with the Greek social security system. Such exemptions may be granted for one year and may be reviewed annually for a further two years. The exemption depends on the nature of the work being done, *eg* employment for the purpose of training local employees, installing new equipment, supervising a re-organisation, or for other special needs. The exemption is generally not granted where the foreigner, although temporarily assigned to Greece, is employed in a position of a permanent nature.

Prescribing drugs

Greek pharmacists are well trained and dispense a number of medicines which elsewhere could only be prescribed by a doctor. In the larger towns there will usually be one that speaks good English. Homeopathic and herbal remedies are quite widely available, with homeopathic pharmacies in many of the larger towns. Note that the well trained pharmacists are also authorised to give injections if they deem the treatment appropriate.

Importing medicines

If you use any form of prescription drug in the UK regularly, you should bring to Greece a copy of the prescription together with the generic name of the drug — this will help should you need to replace it and also avoid possible problems with Customs officials. It is worth noting that codeine is banned in Greece. If you import any, even the common American empirin-codeine compound, you run the risk of receiving a heavy fine. Check all labels on bottles very carefully.

Buying contraceptive pills

Contraceptive pills are bought over the counter at any *farmakío*. No questions asked and they are extremely cheap. They are becoming more readily available as each year passes, but don't count on local availability — unfortunately abortion is still the principal form of birth control. A wide range of condoms, however, is available cheaply. Just ask for *profilaktiká* at any pharmacy or kiosk *(períptero)*.

Going to the dentist

Provided you hold the form E111, you will be directed to a dentist who works for the social insurance scheme. Ask him to treat you under the IKA scheme. You will not be charged. If you are given a prescription take it to any chemist *farmakío* where you will pay 25 per cent of the cost of the medication. The *farmakío* is clearly marked by a red or green cross on a white background.

Thinking about facilities for the disabled

It is usually best to get a medical certificate of fitness to travel provided by a doctor before setting off for Greece. You should consider making a list of all the facilities that will make your life easier whilst you are in Greece and discuss the implications with appropriate officials. You should ask yourself the following ten simple questions:

1. Do I need accommodation on the ground floor, and is it easily found?

2. Are there large lifts available to take me to second and subsequent floors of buildings that I need to visit?

3. Can I get around safely in a wheelchair?

4. How happy am I that weather will not affect my disability?

5. Where do I go for my specially prescribed medication? Can I guarantee a supply?

6. Is there any special needs nursing care available locally?

7. Will I need to take specially adapted clothing and equipment? Are they hard to get in Greece?

8. Will I have any language problems?

9. Is there a relevant association or body of people who can help me in Greece?

10. What do I need to take with me that I can't get in Greece?

CASE STUDIES

Graham breaks an arm

In the idle pursuit of fruit picking in Crete, Graham manages to fall out of a tree in Heraklion. It is immediately evident that his arm is broken and will need setting. His employer kindly offers to drive Graham to the nearby state hospital (*yenikó nosokomio*). Unfortunately, one look at the rows of injured tourists and locals, some sitting and some lying on stretchers, confirms Graham's worst fear that as a minor case he is in for quite a wait. Eventually, after almost five hours, he is seen by a doctor who has his arm set in plaster immediately. Graham loses a day's wages but is grateful that he is not working in a particularly rural location.

Tony and Wendy see red

As teachers, Tony and Wendy are well aware of their employment rights. When Wendy falls pregnant with her second child, she immediately goes to the headmaster to discuss maternity leave. Initially, the headmaster is not prepared to keep Wendy's job open while she has the baby. However, after a meeting with a kindly official at the British Consulate in Athens, and a subsequent exchange of correspondence, the headmaster is persuaded to be reasonable, and with good grace complies with the welfare legislation which states that employers may not terminate the employment of pregnant women.

John and Betty learn about health forms

John and Betty were informed back in the UK that as pensioners they are entitled to free medical treatment. This is all well and good until Betty tries to obtain medication for her arthritis from the local *farmakío*. Despite proof that she is a pensioner, the chemist insists on production of the necessary health form which gives evidence of the previous free treatment in the UK. Betty is requested to visit her local IKA office and obtain the E121 form before the chemist hands out the free medication. This she duly does, picking one up for John at the same time to prevent the same shenanigans when her husband needs medication.

POINTS TO CONSIDER

1. Think closely about the benefits that private health care would afford you and your family. Do you really want to be subjected to long waits in large state hospitals? Are you prepared for the lack of nursing care in state hospitals?

2. Check out the locations of hospitals, doctors, dentists and pharmacists before you decide to rent or buy a property. Are you sure that adequate health facilities are nearby in the case of an emergency?

3. Don't be afraid to quiz pharmacists on what they are prepared to dispense without a prescription. This knowledge will stand you in good stead and prevent hours of waiting to see doctors, dentists *etc* if it is not really necessary.

8

Working for a Living

Although any subject of an EU country does not theoretically require a work permit, in practice a lot of temporary work is administered on an *ad hoc* basis with a blind eye often turned by officialdom and employers alike to the status of the employee. The legal minimum age for employment in Greece is 15 years. Women and young people should not be engaged in dangerous jobs.

REGISTERING YOUR DETAILS

Put simply, to work in Greece you must have a full passport, a temporary or excursion passport will not suffice. You are free to enter Greece for up to three months in order to seek work or establish a business. As discussed earlier in Chapter 5, even if you are visiting Greece to look for work, you may be asked *ad infinitum* to prove that you are financially independent and have the finances to return to the UK if need be.

FINDING WORK

As a UK/EU national, you have the right to live and work in Greece without a work permit, sharing the same rights as Greek nationals for pay, working conditions, access to housing, vocational training, social security and trade union membership. Your families and immediate dependants are entitled to join you and enjoy similar rights. However, there is a difference between theory and practice and you will find that a work permit is often expected. Beware the unscrupulous employers who will have you believe that, without a work permit, you are operating illegally and therefore the rate of pay will be depressed to compensate for the employers' risk.

Making the most of the network

The Government Employment Service in each member country of the

EEA (European Union countries, Norway and Iceland) publish details of vacancies supplied via the EURES network. EURES is a partnership of all the employment services in the EEA, to promote free movement of workers. This network is fully computerised allowing access of up to date information on living and working conditions in each EEA member state. There are over 500 specially trained staff who update the information; they are called Euroadvisers and specialise in local employment issues. The EURES website is: *http://europa.eu.int/jobs/eures*. Also see Useful Addresses.

Visiting youth hostels
Surprisingly, this is an extremely good source of local knowledge, mostly for casual and seasonal work. You would always hope to run into English speaking Europeans in a similar situation to your own.

Assessing job centres
UK/EU nationals also have free access to the services of the Greek employment service, which is managed by the Manpower Employment Organisation *Organisimos Apasholisseos Ergatikou Dynamikou* (OAED). The address of the nearest post office can be found in the telephone directory (*tilephonikos odigos*). Further information required that cannot be provided by your nearest OAED should be addressed to the European Employment Services section at OAED head office (see Useful Addresses).

Contacting private agencies
With few exceptions, private employment agencies are forbidden by law in Greece. Those allowed to operate are called *Grafía Evrésseos Ergassías* and are listed under that heading in the Greek equivalent of *Yellow Pages, Chryssos Odigos*. Some UK employment agencies which deal with work abroad are registered with the Federation of Recruitment and Employment Services Limited (FRES). If you write to FRES outlining the type of employment you are looking for, they may be able to provide a list of suitable agencies that are licensed by the Department of Employment (see Useful Addresses or website at *www.rec.uk.com*). There may be a notional charge for this service.

Getting further information
A useful directory for professionals, executives and managers is the *CPEC Recruitment Guide* which lists recruitment agencies and search consultants in the UK. Many of these deal with overseas assignments

EXPERIENCED Filipino couple for housekeeping required by 3 persons in villa. Excellent salary according to experience 200.000-250.000 each + IKA. ☎8843.123, 5 Ipirou, 2nd floor, "Estia", 9-3 (OMT682)

EXPERIENCED hairdressers (male/female) up to 28 y.o. to work in "Metallax" hairdressing salon in Voula. Salary 200.000 and IKA and bonus. Good prospects. Also manicure & make-up specialists up to 22 y.o. ☎8955.144 (A)

FEMALE employees 25-35 years old, speaking English or Greek for an exchange company in Mykonos ☎0289.28157/28158 (A5974)

FILIPINO - Sri Lankan lady up to 40 yrs old is required as live-in housekeeper in Ekali. Experience with children necessary ☎0972.559461 (A5973)

FILIPINO girl required to live in. ☎8994.028 (E1255)

GOOD-LOOKING lady, 20-30 y.o. needed as live-in househelper. Salary 260.000 + bonus. Excellent conditions. ☎7565.361, 17.00-22.00 Alex (A5870)

INDIA people for company, secretaries, chartering experienced persons, captains for shies and chemist, medicine persons ☎0945.422365 (OM309)

LIVE-IN Filipino woman up to 45 years old as housekeeper. Experience mandatory and able to communicate in Greek language. Salary 220.000 and IKA and bonus. ☎7232.614 (A)

LIVE-IN Filipino woman up to 45 years old as housekeeper. Experience mandatory and able to communicate in Greek language. Salary and IKA. ☎7797.063 (9-3pm) (A5964)

LIVE-IN home and kid help required in Maroussi. Female, under 35, non-smoker, recommendations. ☎0944.271709 (M1138)

LIVE-IN maid for family in Kalamaki. ☎9852.823 or 097.2321232

LS PUBLISHERS. We are an expanding company speacialising in English language teaching material and are looking for creative EFL teachers to join our editorial department. The right candidate should: be a British native speaker, hold a university degree, have at least five years' experience of teaching in Greece, possess good writing skills. Candidates can apply by sending their CV by fax (5769.667), e-mail: (lamda@hol.gr). Attn: Frosso Tabaki ☎5779.532 (AT4730)

NANNY - au pair wanted for 3 1/2 year old boy and 8 month old girl. Live-on cycladic island. Accommodation provided ☎0286.91472

SITUATIONS VACANT

A couple and a single lady, Greek or foreigners, are asked for internal housekeepers in a residence at Filothei. Previous experience at least five years and references are necessary. Good salary and insurance.

Tel: 3473000, Mrs Anastasopoulou

A WELL KNOWN PLASTIC SURGERY seeks to appoint A PLASTIC COORDINATOR

young lady up to 35. Pleasant personality, excellent communication skills. Experience in MD's office/clinic/hospital environment will be ideal (3-5 years). Computer-literate, good command of English. Send detailed CV (recent photo necessary): P.O. Box 62058, 15210 Halandri

EXPERIENCED Filipino couple for housekeeping required by 3 persons in villa. Excellent salary according to experience 200.000-250.000 each + IKA. ☎8843.123, 5 Ipirou, 2nd floor, "Estia", 9-3

EXPERIENCED hairdressers (male/female) up to 28 y.o. to work in "Metallax" hairdressing salon in Voula. Salary 200.000 and IKA and bonus. Good prospects. Also manicure & make-up specialists up to 22 y.o. ☎8955.144

FILIPINO lady as live-in housekeeper. Greek language and previous experience required. Salary 200.000 drs and IKA and bonus. ☎7232.614

FILIPINO woman, serious, good-mannered, reliable, gentle with children, to live-in with respectable 3-member family in Kifissia. Salary and days-off negotiable. Day phone ☎6425.890, evening phone 8000.501, mobile ☎0944.330866

LIVE-IN couple required, experienced huosekeepers/cook/garden/motor yacht, separate house. Place: Aghia Marina/Lagonissi. Able to communicate in Greek. Age: 25-40. ☎9852.333, 0977.282831 Mrs Maria

LIVE-IN Filipino woman up to 45 years old as housekeeper. Experience mandatory and able to communicate in Greek language. Salary 220.000 and IKA and bonus. ☎7232.614

LIVE-IN maid for family in Kalamaki. ☎9852.823 or 097.2321232

NATIVE English teachers required for language school in Ghyzi area, for summer and winter courses. 2600 drs per hour. Contact number ☎6432.264, from 10.30 am to 12 noon

TOURISTIC shop in Monastiraki needs a saleswoman, foreign languages speaker. Greek language necessary. ☎3213.124 (A5945)

YOUNG ladies 18-28 y.o. required to work in a disco-bar in Tolo. ☎0752.59505

NATIVE English speaking lady to look after a 2 year old boy (afternoon hours). ☎6718.951 hours 10-1, 6-9 (OMT681)

PART-TIME accountant required for professional office all overseas business. EPE company, with Cypriot holding company, based in Nea Erithrea. English is essential. Please apply in writing with short CV days & time available and salary wanted. P.O. Box 51311, Kifissia 145 10, ☎6250.563-4 after 4pm daily - Ms. Sayed (A5940)

SECRETARY bilingual (excellent knowledge of English and Greek) is required for an SA company in Athens. Skills must include typing, Word. Summer vacations on August. ☎3634.283, 10am-4pm (A5957)

URGENTLY required: receptionist lady speaking English and PC literate. Also athletic gentleman required speaking English, must be good swimmer. ☎8843.123, 5 Ipirou, 2nd floor, "Estia" Mon-Fri

YOUNG ladies 18-28 y.o. required to work in a disco-bar in Tolo. ☎0752.59505 (A5939)

ALL AGES of good looking people & kids are needed for TV commercials & modelling work ☎6856.200 (AT4647)

AN INTERNATIONAL trading company seeks a system administrator with experience in WIN NT, Linux & MS Access, to have knowledge in accounting and to be fluent in English. The company offers a good remuneration package. If interested please fax your CV in English to fax no. ☎9249.249, ref. ACP (KT360)

EFL ORGANISATION in Kallithea requires professional experienced English (Greek) secretaries & teachers. References necessary. ☎9568.833 (KT359)

ENGLISH live-in/out lady required to look after a 13 y.o. girl ☎0944.533313 (E1254)

ENGLISH native speaking girl requested for baby sitting, full-time, live-in at Agios Stefanos. ☎4836.321 (8.00-16.00) (A5946)

Fig. 13. A selection of situations vacant.

and some have offices abroad. Your local public reference library may have this guide. It can also be purchased directly from the authors (see Useful Addresses). Job centre vacancies (including those for work overseas) are also advertised on the Internet at *www.employmentservice.gov.uk*

Using the press

Major newspapers including *Ta Nea, Eleftheros Tipos, Eleftherotipia* and *Apogevmatini* all carry job pages. Word of mouth remains a very powerful medium for job hunting in Greece.

An English language newspaper, *Athens News*, also carries vacancies (see Figure 13). Vacancies sometimes also appear in the UK press but these are usually with UK based companies. International newspapers such as the *European* and the *International Herald Tribune* carry managerial, technical and other professional staff vacancies. Professional journals and magazines available in the UK may also be a useful source of jobs, especially if a journal is world renowned. *Benns Media*, a directory listing all UK trade magazines and journals, is available in public reference libraries.

You can also advertise yourself in newspapers by either contacting the newspaper direct or using an agency such as *Publicitas* (see Useful Addresses).

Writing to professional associations and unions

Another source of contacts could be the professional association or union that you may belong to. Such organisations may well have contacts with counterparts in Greece who could provide information useful to your job search. The directory *Trade Associations and Professional Bodies of the UK* may be useful in this respect. This directory should be available at a local public reference library.

Finding Chambers of Commerce

This is a possible source of company information. For further information on UK companies operating in Greece contact the British Chamber of Commerce in Athens or Thessaloniki (see Useful Addresses).

ASSESSING THE WORK AVAILABLE

Generally speaking, you would be interested in either short term or more permanent work. Short term or casual/seasonal work is greatly affected by supply and demand of jobs to be done and labour available.

EXAMINING SHORT TERM OPPORTUNITIES

With the recent flood of Albanians and other Eastern Europeans into Greece, unskilled labour rates have become very depressed due to the huge pool of labour available. However, some perennial jobs are always available. A little digging and asking around should provide openings in:

- bar work
- waiting in a *tavérna* or *kafenió*
- harvesting fruit and vegetables
- building repairs and upkeep
- camp site assistance
- busking
- making and selling giftware
- voluntary work.

In addition, information about seasonal and casual work can be found in several excellent books dedicated to working abroad. Check with reference libraries: failing that a list of good books can be found in Further Reading.

Working in a bar

Just wander around the streets asking in the bars and pretty soon you will find something. Women always succeed where men quite often fail. The hours are long, pay is poor and job security is zero. Watch out for immoral proposals from the owner!

Waiting on table

One rung up the ladder from bar work is waiting and serving. Pay is generally improved as you will be expected to earn most of it in tips. If you're lucky you may get free food and sometimes free lodgings thrown in. Some knowledge of Greek is useful.

Harvesting fruit and vegetables

Unlike bar work, agricultural jobs can mainly go to the men. Watch out for the canny farmers who may try it on and pay women at a lower rate per hour for the same work as their male friends. Although predominantly summer and autumn seasonal work, you can work year round if you are prepared to move around the country. A possible calendar of agricultural work, though by no means exhaustive, could include harvesting:

- winter (November - February)
  — oranges in Náfplio
  — lemons in Spárti
  — olives in Peloponnese

- spring (March - April)
  — potatoes in Kalamáta
  — artichokes in Toló
  — tomato growing in Crete

- summer (May - September)
  — cherries in Trípolis
  — pears in Argos
  — apricots in Náfplio
  — watermelons in Kalamáta
  — potatoes in Crete
  — peaches in Thessaloniki
  — walnuts, almonds in Peloponnese

- autumn (October - November)
  — apples in Pirgos
  — raisins in Trípolis
  — grape picking in Trípolis
  — strawberries in Náxos.

Use your common sense to get work. If the fruit looks ripe on the trees it will need to be picked. Find the land owner, get the best piece rate you can and try to include accommodation for your stay.

Repairing pensions, hotels and other facilities

This is mainly done outside the tourist season, when the weather is milder. Getting ready for the season involves painting, repairing and making everywhere look spick and span. Quite often boat yards and yacht marinas need casual help to repaint and refit vessels before the new season.

Helping out on campsites

Tourist related work, such as washing up, is always needed at campsites, bars, restaurants *etc*. This is a good opportunity to mix with other Northern Europeans who quite often pass on good tips for better paid and immediately available work. Cleaning out toilets, long hours in reception and sorting out pitches for that night's campers and caravanners are all par for the course.

Busking

Well, if you've got talent fine, otherwise stick to washing up. The Athens underground is popular and purportedly rich in pickings. In fashionable resorts you can quite often get hired as a travelling musician to appear nightly in pubs and hotels as part of an entertainment programme.

Selling your wares

Living on your own initiative, being creative with wood, paper, clay *etc* and reselling to the general public can be very lucrative. You could consider importing items on a small scale, *eg* clothing, jewellery and other fashion items, and selling them on to market traders at a profit. The problem here is that you need available capital to invest. Obviously a basic knowledge of Greek and a sound understanding of the principles of haggling is imperative.

Working as a volunteer

It is normally best to approach specialist agencies in the UK to discuss specific opportunities. See Further Reading for publications. In the main the work is project based, quite often from a charitable foundation. Currently volunteers are required to act as wildlife guides accompanying British school parties, helping to run an outdoor adventure centre for disabled children and restoring a traditional village. The well advertised Trireme Trust always needs keen, fit and healthy volunteers to help row and maintain a reconstruction of an ancient Greek sailing ship.

Pros and cons of casual work

Pros

- Flexibility — you work the hours and days to suit.

- Variety — the chance to move around Greece at will and try your hand at many jobs.

- Sociability — an easy way of meeting people of different nationalities from all walks of life.

Cons

- Poor pay — you could be exploited by unscrupulous employers.

- Availability — sometimes due to an excess of labour you will go weeks without finding something.

- Legislation — quite often casual work is obtained without work permits, employers turning a blind eye to deduction of taxation and IKA *etc.*

INVESTIGATING LONGER TERM EMPLOYMENT

With language as a potential barrier, you have to decide on what particular talents you offer the marketplace, before seeking a more permanent job. However, the more popular and easily available job roles traditionally include:

- teaching
- nursing
- au pair.

Teaching English

There is considerable demand for the teaching of English as a foreign language, and there are many opportunities for regular and part-time employment. However, prospective employees should examine contracts carefully before taking up a post. A Presidential Decree signed in 1997 made it possible for the EU nationals to be generally employed in, and also open, language schools *(frontistiria)*. To get a job in a school you need to have a TEFL (teaching of English as a foreign language certificate) or a university degree (preferably in English). Speaking Greek helps but is not essential, although there are now certain certification criteria regarding a basic knowledge of the Greek language. Relevant examinations for obtaining such certificates can be sat under the jurisdiction of the Ministry of Education (see Useful Addresses).

The simplest way to get a teaching job is to apply before leaving — preferably in Britain. There are advertisements published weekly, particularly from August to October, in the *Guardian* newspaper. Quite often teachers are able to supplement their incomes by providing private lessons to pupils in their homes. This can be lucrative. Officially you need a teaching permit, but teachers seldom bother.

Nursing

Qualified nurses wishing to take up employment in Greece should write before arriving in Greece directly to the Association of Graduate Nurses — details in Useful Addresses. Vacancies exist at the larger private hospitals in the bigger towns. English is always spoken and the level of nursing care high. The RGN Council in the UK also has an Overseas Liaison Officer who can offer practical advice.

Au pair work

The popularity and scale of private English teaching also means that English speaking women are heavily in demand as au pairs. As ever, such positions tend to be exploited and low paid, but if you can use them to your own ends living reasonably well and learning Greek there can be mutual benefits.

Being cautious

It is unwise to arrange anything until you are in Greece so you can at least meet and talk terms with your prospective family. In Athens in particular you should have little difficulty in finding a good family. Posts are advertised in the daily *Athens News* and there are quite a number of specialist news agencies. Details of a few are in Useful Addresses.

WORKING CONDITIONS

The five day, 40 hour week is normal in both private and public sectors. You may be requested by your employer to work overtime in cases of urgent deadlines or if special work makes this necessary. The traditional siesta time (2.30 pm - 5 pm) is still adhered to on most of the islands and out in the country, although it is not so popular now in the European orientated larger towns and cities. All employees are entitled to join trade unions and go on strike in order to pursue their civil law rights.

Complying with legal overtime

Overtime of up to 120 hours in a calendar year, for which the approval of the Labour Office has been obtained and certain normal formalities have been complied with, is called legal overtime and is paid at the premium of 25 per cent for up to 60 hours per year, 50 per cent for 60–120 hours per year and 75 per cent for over 120 hours per year.

Working illegal overtime

Overtime which is worked without complying with any of the

previously mentioned formalities is called illegal overtime and is compensated by an additional amount of 100 per cent of normal hourly salary.

Checking your holiday allowance

If you are on a five day week and have completed one year of employment, annual vacation is set at 20 working days, increasing to 21 days after two years of service, and 22 days for three years of service and more.

Understanding salaries

Salaries are normally quoted on a monthly basis. In addition to the twelve monthly salaries payable in the year, an additional month's salary is normally payable as a Christmas bonus, an additional half a month's salary is normally payable as an Easter bonus and an additional half a month's salary is normally payable as vocational allowance, or summer bonus.

Dismissals

An employer must pay severance compensation to dismissed employees based on their salary at time of dismissal and their years of service. Severance compensation increases from one month's salary for employees with one year of service or less, to six months' salary for employees with ten years of service. For each year of service in excess of ten years, one extra month's salary is paid up to a maximum of 24 months' salary.

Avoiding dismissal

Organisations employing up to 50 employees can normally dismiss up to five per month. However, those employing more than 50 workers are entitled to dismiss two to three per cent of the work force but not exceeding a maximum of 30 per month. The Ministry of Labour determines the specified percentage which varies from time to time.

SELECTING A JOB FROM THE UK

If you are able, through exchanges of correspondence, to secure a job in Greece from the UK, then you should make doubly sure to obtain a written statement/agreement detailing the job offer and specifying minimum terms. Before you take up employment ensure that you:

- Become competent in Greek, or improve the competence you already have.

- Go to your local social security office and find out what rules will apply if you visit Greece to look for work.

- Have a copy of the contract or terms and conditions of employment and ensure you understand them fully. (Hours of work, termination clauses *etc.*)

- Have a full UK/EU passport.

- Have accommodation in the area you will be moving to.

- Have the E111 medical expenses cover or have taken out some private health insurance.

- Have sufficient funds to last until you are paid, or to return home if necessary.

- Know the method and frequency of payment of any salary.

- Know what travel arrangements need to be made and whether you or the employer will pay.

- Make arrangements with people in your own country who can serve as references for potential employers in Greece.

- Take out a travel insurance policy that covers luggage, accidents and personal liability.

- Try to obtain copies of the major Greek daily newspapers to see if there are any jobs you can apply for before leaving.

- Understand who is paying the fares to and from Greece.

CASE STUDIES

Graham heads North

After finally arriving in Thessaloníki after two days' hitchhiking, Graham decides to look around for work. He has heard that the olive harvesting season is just beginning and that casual workers are required. He waits at dawn for the farmer's trucks to arrive, only to discover when they do that hordes of Albanians clamber on board, leaving him no space. Undeterred, he decides to walk around the bars, building sites and tourist shops seeking work. Eventually he is offered washing up at a nearby *tavérna*. The hours are anti-social, 9 pm to 3 am, the pay is pitiful, but at least he has his days to himself for exploring the area and one good meal during his shift.

Tony and Wendy land on their feet
It has always been Tony and Wendy's intention to give up their teaching posts in England and travel overland to teach English as a foreign language. After arriving in Athens and registering their accommodation details with the British embassy, they are introduced to the secretary of the British Hellenic Chamber of Commerce, who kindly lends them the *Members Business Directory*. From this they are able to track down the reputable foreign language schools, and soon afterwards find available posts. In contrast to other administrative headaches they have encountered along the way, obtaining gainful employment proves to be straightforward and problem free.

John and Betty supplement their income
Despite being pensioners, John and Betty feel they ought to get some part time work to help pay the household bills. On their lovely island of Skíathos, they soon discover that any work other than washing up, bar work or waiting on tables is hard to come by. By chance one day, they are strolling along a favourite stretch of coastal road when they happen to fall upon a yacht chandlers and boat yard. Asking inside, they are delighted when John is offered some boat refurbishing work, light carpentry and joinery which suits him fine, and Betty is enticed to help out in the office. As neither of them have work permits, they keep a low profile and enjoy the pin money they receive.

POINTS TO CONSIDER

1. How tied down do you want to be in a job? Is it worth getting lower paid casual work to keep the options open for moving on?

2. How happy are you to accept low wages and anti-social hours in order to make enough to pay the bills and travel, or do you want to put down roots with more permanent employment?

3. How do you feel about working in a hot climate when everyone else is on holiday? Can you buckle down to a regular regime?

9

Doing Business

Since 1 January 1981, UK/EU nationals have had the right to be self employed in Greece. In certain professions, for example teaching, the Greek authorities may require you to satisfy minimum British Council qualifications and other requirements. Consequently, if you are contemplating becoming a self employed teacher, it would be worthwhile discussing the practical requirements with the necessary authorities, *ie* Greek embassy in London or OAED offices in Greece, before commencement. Interestingly, less than 5 per cent of the working population of some four-and-a-half million are unemployed and of those in work just under one third are women.

Being punctual
Greek businessmen do not have a good reputation for punctuality. While it is best for you to be on time for meetings yourself, you should be prepared for a wait. Quite often if an appointment is arranged for say 10.00 am, this is the time that the person you are due to meet is likely to leave their office for the appointment, as opposed to the time you expect them to be with you.

Playing the bureaucratic game
Bureaucracy — the Greeks invented the word and love the pastime. You will soon discover that Greeks are suspicious by nature, particularly regarding your business affairs. With endless visits to various government departments on apparently fruitless trips, you will soon get used to the real or perceived obstacles put in the way of your progress.

SETTING UP A BUSINESS
You should follow these four simple steps if you are looking to start a business in Greece:

1. Obtain a residence permit from the Aliens Bureau.

2. Register with the local tax office. You will receive advice on the type of accounting books that need to be kept, rates of taxation *etc.*

3. Register with the local Chamber of Commerce and Industry. You will be asked to pay a subscription and a deposit. Both these sums are fixed by the Chamber. Proof that you have registered with your local Chamber and with the appropriate professional association is mandatory. You will be asked when you visit the tax office.

4. Depending on the type of work you are proposing to set up, you should register with the local Artisans and Tradesmen's Insurance fund (TEVE) or the local Merchants Insurance fund (TAE). If you can provide a certificate showing that you are registered with a state insurance organisation back in the UK, this may dispense with a need to register with a Merchants Insurance fund.

These Greek laws and regulations apply to both Greek and foreign nationals — you're not being picked on!

Obtaining further information

Further detailed information on the legislation, and on the regulations governing the setting up of a business in Greece, can be obtained from Greek commercial lawyers and accountants (see Useful Addresses). It is strongly recommended that professional advice should be obtained, particularly where you wish to set up a limited liability company (SA).

CONSIDERING TYPES OF BUSINESS

There are numerous ways in which a foreign business can be established and operated in Greece. The main forms are:

*   working for yourself as a sole trader
*   joining other people in partnership
*   acting as a branch of an overseas organisation
*   registering as a Law 89 company
*   forming a limited liability company
*   trading as a corporation
*   establishing a joint venture.

Setting up as a sole trader

This is by far the simplest form of business where you carry on business in your own name and are personally responsible for all debts. You are required to file your accounts annually to 31 December.

Registering for IKA

If you are self employed you may be exempt from paying Greek social security contributions (*IKA*) for up to twelve months, providing you continue to pay UK national insurance and hold the exemption certificate E101. This form E101 is issued by the overseas branch of the Department of Social Services — see Useful Addresses.

Pros and cons of working for yourself

Pros

● Flexibility — you can establish where you work, when you work and, depending on the hours and effort you put in, how much profit you make.

● Regional grants — if you pick the geographic location and type of business carefully you can enjoy substantial government aid.

● Kudos — there is considerable self-respect and satisfaction to be found in establishing a small business. The local Greek community will admire you for it.

Cons

● Bureaucracy — initially you will have to put up with endless visits to the authorities to register your papers, and numerous visits from the police whilst they establish that you are setting up a *bona fide* business.

● Taxation — you will really need to understand this complex subject matter to avoid being inadvertently caught out. Good sound professional advice is recommended.

● Exposure — as you are responsible for 'bringing home the bacon', it is entirely up to you to ensure that your source of work does not dry up, as your overheads will still need to be paid. As it is very difficult to get a bank overdraft in Greece, and expensive, you will need to trade within your own capital resources.

Forming a partnership

A general partnership (*omorythmos eteria* OE) is an entity in which the partners agree to be jointly and severally liable for the debts of the partnership. A partnership deed needs to be drawn up, signed by all partners and formally filed with the First Instance Court as a legally binding contract.

There is no minimum requirement for the formation of a partnership. This liability is unlimited regardless of the capital introduced by the individuals. However, it is possible to form a limited liability partnership (*eterorryhtmi eteria,* EE) in which the limited partners are only responsible for liabilities incurred by the partnership up to the amount of their capital contribution.

Representing an overseas company

A permit from the Ministry of Commerce is required if you are considering acting as an agent or branch representative of a UK or EU based organisation (*ipokastastimata*). You will need to present the following documents:

- A certificate by the appropriate authority in the country of origin that the company continues operations.

- Copy of the company's Certificate of Incorporation and statutes, and the names of the persons who are buying the company and the country of origin.

- Copy of the Power of Attorney in favour of the foreign company's representative in Greece.

- Resolution of the overseas company for the establishment of a branch in Greece.

A branch may be registered as a corporation limited by shares, or as a branch of a foreign limited company. In either case the company must show proof that its capital is not less than 20 million GRD or 6 million GRD respectively.

Foreign companies with a branch in Greece must file a copy of their annual accounts together with a statement of operations, translated into Greek, with the Ministry of Commerce within three months after approval at the annual general meeting.

Floating an offshore company

Legislation exists to permit foreign commercial, industrial and shipping enterprises to establish a branch or an office in Greece for the purpose of co-ordinating or monitoring the business of the entity outside Greece or for high level supervision of a Greek subsidiary. These organisations are known as Law 89 companies (*grafia nomou 89*). The benefits of this legislation are:

● duty free importation of private cars
● exemption from complying with limit on overtime working hours
● exemption from Greek income tax
● exemption from various indirect taxes
● right to employ an unlimited number of foreign personnel in the business.

The main condition for establishing a branch or office under this law is that it must exclusively be engaged on business activities outside of Greece. Such an enterprise must import at least US$74,000 or the equivalent in other currencies each year to meet its operating expenses in Greece.

Forming a limited liability company

A limited liability company (*eteria periorismenis efthynis,* EPE) is similar to a partnership with a limited liability.

A limited liability company is established by notarial act which contains the statutes, which must be published in the *Government Gazette.* The main items that must be included are:

● date of formation
● its issued and fully paid up share capital
● its registered office
● its trading objectives
● name of company secretary
● names of shareholders
● the name of the company.

A limited liability company must have a minimum share capital of 6 million GRD. This capital is divided into share certificates of at least 10,000 GRD. The members of a limited liability company are surprisingly called partners. Every one of them is liable for the debts of the company up to the amount of their respective share certificates. A limited liability company must consist of at least two partners.

Operating as a sole person limited liability company
It is now possible to establish a sole person limited liability company. The sole partner may be either an individual or a legal person, but the same person cannot be the sole partner in more than one sole person limited liability company.

All the requirements for maintaining books, registering documents *etc* that apply to a limited liability company also apply, but in addition the words 'sole person' must precede the words 'limited liability company'.

Appropriate business decisions of the sole partner must be recorded in a minutes book, countersigned by a notary public in the registered office of the company. Be mindful that the sole person limited liability company is a legal entity separate and distinct from sole partner.

Trading as a corporation

A Greek corporation (*anonymi eteria,* AE) is formed through notarial act. At least two founding members, individuals or legal entities are required. The formation of an AE and its statutes must be legally approved by a government official in which the company's registered office is situated. This registration approving the formation of the company and its statutes must be published in the *Government Gazette.*

The minimum share capital of the corporation is 20 million GRD. The share capital is divided into shares, the domination of which must be at least 100 GRD and not higher than 30,000 GRD. The share capital of the corporation must be fully paid up to at least the amount of the minimum capital requirement. If the share capital is in excess of the minimum capital requirement, payment of the amount in excess may be paid over a period not exceeding ten years provided that the shares remain registered until fully paid.

Managing a corporation
The affairs of a corporation are managed by a board of directors consisting of at least three members. The board members may delegate the day to day running of the affairs of the corporation to one of their members, who is called the managing director. The directors must meet at least once a month, and in order to have a quorum the majority of directors must be present in person. A general meeting must be held at least once a year and within six months from the end of the financial year.

Establishing a joint venture

Under Greek law joint ventures (*kinopraxia*) are not recognised as separate legal entities. Therefore each participant of a joint venture is liable for his share of the total debts. For tax purposes, though, a joint venture is treated as a legal entity and a 35 per cent tax is imposed on the profits made.

COMPLYING WITH THE LEGISLATION

Unlike the UK, there are different methods of dealing with year end affairs.

Distributing profits

At least five per cent of the year's after tax profit must be transferred annually to a statutory reserve until the reserves represent one third of the share capital. Of the remaining profits, a dividend of at least six per cent of the paid up capital or 35 per cent of the net profit reduced by the amount transferred to the statutory reserve, whichever is greater, must be paid.

Reporting requirements

The books and records that must be kept by all trading entities in Greece are listed in the Books and Records Code, in three categories. The organisation's turnover determines the relevant category as follows:

- First category books (turnover up to 25 million GRD) simply comprises a purchase day book in which all purchases must be recorded in a set manner.

- Second category books (turnover up to 300 million GRD) comprises an income and expense book in which the organisation's turnover from the sale of goods and services as well as purchases and general expenses must be recorded in a pre-set manner.

- Third category books (for turnover greater than 300 million GRD) comprises a full set of books kept on the traditional double entry book-keeping method. Corporations and limited liability companies must keep third category books irrespective of their turnover. In addition, organisations with turnover in excess of 900 million GRD in retail sales or wholesale revenues of 650 million GRD must keep stock records with details regarding quantity and value, together with a formal annual stock take.

Submitting your accounts

All book-keeping records must be approved by the tax authorities before use. Limited liability companies must publish their annual financial statements in the *Government Gazette* and also in certain newspapers — one political and one financial. Copies of financial statements do not need to be submitted to the Ministry of Commerce or any other regulatory body.

As previously mentioned, foreign entities operating through branches in Greece must file a copy of their annual financial statements duly translated into Greek with the Ministry of Commerce together with a summary statement of the branch operations in Greece.

PAYING TAXES

The main taxes in Greece are:

- capital gains tax
- car circulation tax
- income tax
- inheritance and gift taxes
- real estate transfer tax
- tax on ships
- value added tax (VAT or *FPA*).

Paying capital gains tax (CGT)

Capital gains tax is levied on the sale of every fixed or immovable property. The gain on which tax is levied is defined as the difference between the acquisition cost and sale price. Gains from the sale of a business or on the sale of shares of companies not listed on the Athens Stock Exchange are taxed at 20 per cent. Gains from the disposal of other business rights such as patents, industrial property *etc* are taxed at 30 per cent. CGT is primarily, therefore, a business expense. Gains made from the sale of land and buildings are considered to be ordinary income, taxable at the normal income tax rates.

Collecting car circulation tax

An annual circulation tax is imposed on all cars. For private cars, the amount of the tax is based on engine size. The circulation tax is payable in two instalments, the first of which is due by 31 March and the second by 30 September.

Assessing real estate transfer tax

Real estate transfers are generally subject to tax at a rate of 9 per cent on sale prices up to 4 million GRD and 11 per cent on sale prices in excess of that amount. In certain parts of the country these rates are increased by 2 per cent for fire fighting services.

Understanding income tax

Under the Greek income tax laws, an individual's total income must be taxed. This is determined by adding together revenues from all sources and deducting all allowable expenses. Income is classified according to the following source:

- agricultural enterprises
- building rentals
- commercial enterprises
- investment income
- professions and other sources
- salaries and wages.

Electing a financial year

Organisations must elect 30 June or 31 December as their financial year end. An exception to this rule can be made in the case of branches or subsidiaries of foreign companies which may elect the financial year end of their head office or foreign parent after obtaining relevant permission from the tax authorities.

The financial year must cover a twelve month period except in the year of commencement or termination of business which may cover a lesser period.

Taxing of individuals

Every person, irrespective of nationality, domicile or country of residence, is subject to income tax on any revenue arising in Greece. Furthermore, individuals domiciled in Greece are subject to income tax on foreign incomes.

Rules have been established for calculating an individual's income derived from a personal commercial enterprise or profession. In both cases, the objective system of taxation applies where no books or books of a lower category than the third as defined by the Books and Records code are kept. In these cases income is imputed on the basis of living expenditure or acquisition of certain assets. Individuals are then taxed on the higher of their declared income or imputed income.

Fixing taxation rates
Net income after deduction of the allowable expenses is subject to tax as per Figure 14.

Table of Greek Income Tax Payable				
Earnings (GRD) Bracket	% Tax	Tax Per Bracket	Total Income	Cumulative Tax
First 1,600,000	0	0	1,600,000	–
Next 1,110,000	5	55,500	2,710,000	55,500
Next 1,625,000	15	243,750	4,335,000	299,250
Next 3,245,000	30	973,500	7,580,000	1,272,750
Next 8,655,000	40	3,462,000	16,235,000	4,734,750
Over 8,655,000	45			

The nil tax bracket (first bracket) will be increased from 1,600,000 GRD to 2,000,000 GRD for tax year 2000/2001. For employees and pensioners the nil tax bracket is increased from 1,355,000 GRD to 1,900,000 GRD in 2000 and 2,300,00 in 2001.

Fig. 14. Income tax bands.

Filing tax returns
Income tax returns need only be submitted if taxable income exceeds 400,000 GRD, unless all income arises from paid employment in which case the entry level is 800,000 GRD. Personal income tax returns need to be filed by 2 March in the tax year. The net amount of tax is payable in three equal instalments, the first payable no later than the last working day of the month following that in which the assessment is issued.

Imposing inheritance and gift taxes
Inheritance and gift tax is levied on every property, movable or immovable, which passes on death if the property is in Greece. Additionally, moveable property abroad may be subject to inheritance tax if the deceased was a Greek citizen or domiciled in Greece.

Rates of this form of taxation depend on the relationship of the recipient to the deceased. Lower rates are imposed on close family members than on distant relatives or unrelated persons. The tax rates range from 5 to 60 per cent.

The recipient of such an inheritance or gift must file a tax return within six months of the death of the legator, or the publication of the will, or the receipt of the asset.

Taxing ships

Profits arising from the trading of Greek flag ships are exempt from income tax. A special tax based on type of vessel, its age and tonnage is payable instead.

Adding Value Added Tax

Value Added Tax (*Foros Prostithemis Aksias*, FPA) is imposed on the supply of goods and services in Greece, and on goods imported into Greece from other EU countries. The standard rate of VAT is 18 per cent, although a special 8 per cent rate applies to certain necessities including food and pharmaceutical products. A reduced rate of 4 per cent applies to books, newspapers and magazines. VAT is further reduced by 30 per cent if goods or services are supplied to or by taxpayers established in the Dodecanese Islands and other Aegean Islands.

ENCOURAGING INVESTMENT

Greece has actively pursued a policy of attracting foreign investment, particularly in manufacturing, since the 1960s. The Hellenic Industrial Development Bank (ETBA) is the official representative agency. Applications from organisations wishing to set up in Greece and seeking financial support are processed by the Private Investment Directorate of the Ministry of National Economy — see Useful Addresses. Investment in Greece is governed principally by the 1262 Investment Law together with some other measures. These include:

- allowing access to special incentives under the EU's Mediterranean integrated programme
- encouraging off-shore business from foreign companies
- providing special incentives for exporters
- repatriation rights for capital and profits
- tax related incentives for investment.

Obtaining grants

The main investment incentives are:

- accelerated depreciation taxation policy
- cash grants

- creation of tax free reserves
- interest rate subsidies.

In general, such incentives are only available on what is defined as productive investment. Eligible operations include amongst others:

- camp sites
- drying and freezing activities
- energy saving projects
- farming
- fishing
- hotels
- liquid fuel and liquid gas
- manufacturing enterprises
- production
- ship building and repairing
- waste re-processing.

Finding a location

Over half the country's industry is concentrated around Athens, its suburbs and the nearby port of Piraeus. This area contains oil refineries, steelworks, shipyards, and companies producing textiles, chemicals, pharmaceuticals, electrical products, food, beverages and cigarettes. Present policies are aimed at reducing this over-concentration of industry in one area and achieving a better geographical spread. This has further stimulated the already rapid growth of Thessaloníkí into a major industrial centre.

Studying the areas

The availability of government grants is entirely dependent on where in Greece your business is based. The country is split into four sectors on the basis of economic and regional development.

- Area A consists of mainly Athens and Thessaloníkí where grants are only available on a limited range of investments, such as advanced technology, applied research and energy conservation.

- Area B consists of the northern tip of the Peloponnese, north east Athens, Rhodes and Heraklion on the island of Crete.

- Area C encompasses everything not covered by the other three sectors.

● Area D consists of the north eastern districts, the islands near Turkey and a 20km zone along remaining international frontiers except Corfu.

The Hellenic Industrial Bank of Greece (ETBA — see Useful Addresses) publishes excellent guides on availability and location for regional investment. The current grants provided for the four areas and the minimum percentage of own capital participation required in each areas are shown in Figure 15.

	Table of Investment Grants Available			
Area	Industrial, craft industry & mining	Hotels & tourism	Special projects	Minimum participation of investor
A			40%	40%
B	15%	10%	—	40%
C	25%	15%	—	35%
D	35%	25%	—	25%
THRACE	45%	35%	—	15%

Fig. 15. Investment grants available.

CASE STUDIES

Graham uses his initiative

Graham needs to supplement his casual earnings to fund his travelling around Greece. After trying fruit picking, but largely being underbid by the Albanians who were prepared to accept half the wages per day currently paid to the north Europeans, and enjoying only short lived success in the bars where all the work seemed to go to his female counterparts, Graham decides to start his own little business. He casts around for ideas to see what is needed on the island of Póros in the Saronic Gulf where he is currently staying. Gradually, he realises that there is no one cutting tourists' hair. Armed with the knowledge given him by his sister who is a hairdresser back in the UK, and with the sharpest pair of scissors he can obtain, Graham sets up on the harbour wall with just a placard and a smile to promote the business. Very soon, people are queuing for his services – including the local tourist police (*touristikí astinomía*). Graham keeps a list of his daily takings for the authorities to inspect, but he is long gone from Póros before the final day of reckoning.

Tony and Wendy try to comply

After registering with all appropriate authorities in Athens, Tony and Wendy begin their jobs teaching English as a foreign language. Tony has been informed that he needs a copy of his UK teaching certificate and degree papers translated into Greek in order to initially apply for his Greek teaching licence before he can request a residence permit. However, despite spending several mornings at the Ministry of Education it takes him over twelve months before he finally obtains his teaching certificate. During this period, no income tax or national insurance (IKA) has been deducted by his employer, or paid to the taxation authorities. Finally, Tony is presented with a considerable Statement of Deductions Due, covering Wendy's and his own indebtedness for this period, which needs to be paid within 30 days. Luckily enough, Tony and Wendy have been prudent and set this amount aside month by month. Therefore they are able to settle the debt in a timely manner from their savings.

John and Betty get registered

As John and Betty propose to spend more than 185 days a year living in Greece, they find out that they will need to submit an annual tax return to the Greek authorities as residents to cover their income from letting rooms in the old cottage in Skíathos. They diligently keep full details of all takings and expenses in a little red book and make up their first set of accounts to the end of the tax year 31 December. After a few visits by the tourist police (*touristikí astinomía*) to look around and after ensuring that both John and Betty have obtained residence permits, the authorities seem satisfied. Shortly afterwards, John and Betty receive a letter from the Ministry of Finance agreeing their accounts and requiring payment which they duly make. The tourist police continue to visit, but mainly to sample Betty's freshly baked apple pies!

POINTS TO CONSIDER

1. If you are considering forming a partnership, particularly with a Greek, how happy are you to trust the integrity of that person? Remember, you will be jointly and severally liable for the debts of the partnership, not just the debts incurred by yourself.

2. How confident are you of being able to deal with Greek bureaucracy, especially as a sole trader? Are you prepared for endless visits to the Ministry of Finance, being passed from official to official in various departments? Do you really want the Greek tourist police turning up unexpectedly to examine your papers for apparently no reason?

3. What are you going to do if, despite all the waiting and queuing, you are unable to get a residence permit? Consider the implications of starting a business without the appropriate papers of authorisation. How are you going to deal with the taxation authorities? Do you have any contacts at the British consulate or Chamber of Commerce that can help you avoid the anxiety and worry?

10

Education and Recreation

Education in Greece is mandatory for all children between the ages of five and a half and 16. Schools operated by the state are free. Private schools are widely available, primarily in the Athens area servicing the expatriate community. University education is also free.

TRACKING THE EDUCATION PROVIDERS

The types of schooling on offer are:

- primary
- secondary
- college
- universities
- vocational.

Starting at primary school

It is estimated that there are about 10,000 primary schools in Greece catering for almost 1,000,000 children. There are four foreign primary schools in Greece with a Greek educational programme.

St Catherine's British Embassy School, (see Useful Addresses) is the only formally recognised British primary school in Athens. There are no recognised British schools outside Athens, but there are a further eleven primary schools which provide a foreign educational programme *e.g.* American, French, German, Italian, Japanese and Lebanese schools.

Moving on to secondary school

It is believed that there are about 2,100 secondary schools in Greece currently providing education for almost 600,000 pupils. Interestingly enough there are 15 foreign secondary schools providing a Greek educational programme but only a further ten secondary schools operating a foreign educational programme. Almost ten percent of secondary school pupils attend private schools.

The Campion School in Athens (see Useful Addresses) provides an international foundation to its co-educational day school curriculum. It accommodates almost 700 children aged three to 18 from 50 different nationalities. It caters for pupils up to the age of 19 who want to sit GCSE and A levels, as well as the American equivalent CEEB examinations.

Examining higher education opportunities
Higher education includes universities and technical education institutions. There are 17 universities operating today in Greece, covering the full range of theoretical and applied sciences. Many Greek graduates undertake post graduate studies in Greece and abroad.

Receiving vocational training
As an EU national you have the same rights to vocational training as a Greek national. You should contact your nearest local OAED office for further information (see Useful Addresses).

Selecting a school
Picking a school to send your children to can be a tortuous and often hit-and-miss affair. However, there are ways of assessing which school should be best for your particular needs:

● Visit the local British Consul and discuss the various merits of the schools in the area.

● Try and visit a mixture of past and present pupils and parents.

● Ask for a conducted tour of any school that looks interesting. Find out about its history, aims, achievements and problems it may have had. Talk to the staff.

● Read the published prospectus if available.

● Note any schools recommended in authoritative directories e.g. European Council of International Schools.

● Word of mouth – seek to discuss schooling with as many people as you can. Your final decision could affect the wellbeing of your offspring for the next few years.

Finding out about special needs schools

To the best of my knowledge, there is only one recognised school in Athens that caters exclusively for children with special needs. The Old Mill School at Kifissia is a registered trust run by an English headmaster and his dedicated staff to provide full time education for pupils with learning difficulties (see Useful Addresses).

ENJOYING LAND-BASED SPORTS

Numerous health and fitness clubs can be found in the cities and larger towns. Football and basketball are now the largest spectator sports in Greece.

Watching football

Football is by far the most popular sport in Greece, both in terms of participating and watching. The leading teams to watch if you get a chance are Panathanikós and AEK of Athens, Olympiakós of Piraeas and PAOK and Aris of Thessaloniki. Due to the heat football is mostly played in the spring and autumn. League games are played on a Sunday afternoon.

Supporting basketball and volleyball

Basketball has a special place in Greek hearts. Over the years Greece has had some good national teams, but the spectacular defeat of the great Soviet Union in a double foul in overtime that won Greece the Eurobasket Championship in the 1980s truly started the national movement away from football, which had become increasingly corrupt towards the dawn of a new 'clean' sport era. At club level many of the football teams maintain basketball squads to encourage fitness. Thessaloniki houses two of the best teams in the country: PAOK and Aris.

Basketball is certainly a major sport with a lot of television coverage, but volleyball is developing likewise. The European Championships held in Athens a few years ago started the ball rolling, and this has now developed into a very popular sport especially on the beach where permanently erected nets are much in evidence.

Riding horses

There are two excellent riding clubs in Athens; the Hellenic Riding Club and the Athens Riding Club (see Useful Addresses). Most stables get very popular, especially at the weekend so it is well worth booking in advance. Hard hats are not always worn at the stables, so it would be advisable to enquire about the availability of renting or purchasing one. Unfortunately, it is not until you leave the larger cities that you get an opportunity to go on a hack. Within Athens it's mostly riding in a manège.

Hiking

The country offers plenty of rugged terrain for serious hiking and mountaineering. Specialist tour operators in Greece offer guide led tours to some of the remoter parts. See Useful Addresses for details of Greek hiking guides and specialist hiking maps. The Hellenic Alpine Club has situated a refuge hut 6,000 feet up Mount Parnassós, where you can rest for the night before completing your climb to the top (2480 metres). The Greek Mountaineering Federation can provide lists of biking and mountaineering clubs. The Greek Skiing and Alpine Federation maintain in excess of 40 mountain refuge huts, available to its members.

Athletics

The most important race in Greece is the annual Athens Open International Peace Marathon which is held every October. The route tracks the original course ran in 490BC by Pheidippides when he carried the news from Marathon to Athens of victory over the Persians. The finish at the Olympic Stadium in Athens is spectacular.

The 2004 Olympic Games will be staged in Athens which is a blessed relief for the Greeks as they narrowly missed out on hosting the 1996 Olympics, being pipped at the post by a superior bid from Atlanta.

There are running clubs in almost every town in Greece as athletics appeals to the younger keep fit Greeks. If you are based in Athens there is a very active group of Hash Harriers who meet weekly – details in Useful Addresses.

Cycling

Whilst I certainly wouldn't recommend this in Athens, out of the towns this is one of the loveliest ways of exploring the area. The Greek Cycling Federation (see Useful Addresses) can put you in touch with regional cycling clubs.

Hunting

In Greece, hunting is a dubious sport. The Greeks love it, especially getting dressed up in formal hunting gear and setting off for the hills to shoot everything in sight. The official hunting season starts on 20 August or 15 September depending on the area and goes through until the end of March. The most common game hunted includes rabbit, hare, partridge, turtle-dove, quail, duck, geese, fox, wild pig, thrush and woodcock. Two types of hunting licence can be applied for costing less than 20,000 GRD for the season. A Hunting Union exists to regulate the hunting season, types of game and hunting areas.

Exploring underground
Throughout Greece there are thousands of underground caves. The largest are reputedly at Pérama some five kilometres north of Ioannina. They were discovered during the Second World War by a guerilla hiding from the Germans. The Hellenic Speleological Society (see Useful Addresses) can provide details on the best areas in Greece to enjoy the caves.

Following horse racing
Horse racing in Greece is very much a minority sport. The race track in Athens *Ippódromos* is located at the Singroú Delta Faliro racetrack in Tsitsifies. Racing takes place every Monday, Wednesday and Saturday from about 4pm to 8.30pm. On course betting is allowed.

Fishing
The North Aegean islands (Hios, Lésvos, Limnos & Sámos) are recommended for spear fishing. Fishermen report that sea bream, horse mackerel, dorado and blackfish are plentiful. Red mullet is a very common catch and lovely to eat freshly grilled for your dinner. The Amateur Anglers and Maritime Sports Club in Athens (see Useful Addresses), can provide information on facilities available.

Swinging a club
Golfing in Greece is becoming slowly available, but there aren't many 18 hold courses, largely due to the very hot climate preventing good courses being designed and maintained. However, the Glyfada Golf Club near to the old Athens International Airport (see Useful Addresses) is one of the better ones open to the public. Substantial funds have been invested to turn the golf club into a major recreation and leisure venue.

Finding out about tennis
A truly European sport, tennis courts are widely in evidence in the larger towns and cities. The larger hotels mostly have open air courts which are sometimes available to the public. In Athens the Tennis Federation can provide lists of tennis clubs and availability of courts.

MAKING THE MOST OF THE SEA

Well over 3,000 kilometres of Greece is coastline, providing beautiful beaches for sunbathing and sport. Greece does not tend to be blessed with many sandy beaches, shingle and small stones being the norm. However, what it lacks in sand it more than compensates for with thousands of small and sometimes inaccessible coves hidden from view.

Going windsurfing

The last few years have seen tremendous growth in the popularity of wind surfing in Greece. The country's bathing coves are ideal for beginners and boards can usually be hired. Generally speaking, the eastern side of Greece gets the best winds, notably the infamous *meltemi,* which blows incessantly but never seems to reach the western side of the Peloponnese. Particularly good areas include the islands of Lefkádha, Zákinthos, Náxos, Sámos, Lésvos, Corfu, Crete and Methóni in the Peloponnese. The Greek Windsurfing Federation can provide further details on both windsurfing and sail boarding.

Sailing activities

Sail boats and dinghies are rented out by the day or week at many of the country's naval clubs. The International Aegean Sailing week, held in July each year, is the most important regatta in Greece. For information on sailing in Greece contact the Hellenic Professional Yacht Owners Association, the Sailing Federation and the Hellenic Rowing Federation (see Useful Addresses). Water skiing is available at a number of the larger resorts and a fair few of the smaller ones. At many resorts, para-sailing is now available.

Diving for treasure

Due to the risk of theft of submerged antiquities, scuba diving is restricted to a few recognised centres such as the islands of Mikonos, Rhodes, Corfu, Paxi and Lefkáda and on the mainland, the Halkidhiki peninsula. This restriction is an effort to protect Greece's underwater archaeological remains, but recently proposed legislation may lift the ban in order to attract tourists. Initially, if you are considering scuba diving you should make contact with the Underwater Activities Organisation. Even if you have obtained relevant diving certificates of competence, it is illegal to dive on your own in Greece.

Rafting on the rivers

Greece has very powerful white water especially on the Peloponnese and Epirus. Whilst a minority sport, you do occasionally see articles in one of the outdoor magazines e.g. *Korfes*. See Useful Addresses for further details.

Skiing down the mountains

Skiing is a comparative newcomer to Greece, in part because, as you would expect, snow conditions are unpredictable and runs generally short. There are now a dozen ski centres scattered about the mountains. What they lack in professionalism is often made up for by a very easy going and unpretentious ski scene. The cost of skiing is much lower than in Northern Europe. The season generally lasts from the beginning of January to the end of April. The most developed of the resorts is on Parnassós, which is easily accessible from Athens. Throughout the season, the tour operators run buses up to the resort, returning the same day. Surprisingly you can ski as far south as Crete. The Greek Skiing and Alpine Federation will provide listings of good resorts. Once again, details in Useful Addresses.

GETTING OUT AND ABOUT

Largely blessed with a wondrous climate, many outdoor events go on late into the night to take advantage of the cooler air. If you need a baby-sitter for the evening contact the Pan Athenian Union of Baby Sitters (see Useful Addresses).

Pros and cons of living in Athens

Pros

- Accessibility – most European flights arrive at Athens. The port of Piraeus is the departure point for many ferries to the islands.

- Language – English is more widely spoken in Athens than in any other town or city in Greece.

- Employment – you are more likely to get a job as a professional teaching, nursing, au-pairing etc to the rich Greeks in and around Athens than anywhere else.

Cons

- Pollution or *nefos* as the Athenians call it. However, the northern suburbs are less polluted due to their close proximity to the mountains. Needless to say, Athens is bad for anyone with chest complaints.

● Expense – the cost of living, particularly housing is far more expensive than anywhere else in the country.

● Noise – Athens is undoubtedly a very noisy city. Taxis and motorbikes are the worst. With night clubs not closing until the early hours, there is no peace for the wicked.

Dancing the night away

Regular visitors to Greece may have noticed that Greek nightlife is not what it used to be. Bars and discos can no longer stay open all night – the result of controversial measures passed in 1994 to encourage the Greeks to be more alert at work and school the following day. This means that clubs must now shut at 2–3am, although depending on the region and time of year, there may be variations.

From a traditionalist's view point the five best known Greek dances are the *Kalamatiano*, the *Tsamiko*, the *Zeibekiko*, the *Hasapiko* and the *Syrtaki*. Many consider the *Kalamatiano* to be the national dance of Greece. Named after Kalamata, its town of origin, the dance is performed by a number of people moving in a line with each dancer holding his neighbour's hand at shoulder height. The leader weaves intricate patterns of the basic slow-quick-quick-slow step.

Eating out

Dinner in Greece rarely begins before 9.00pm and is likely to go on into the small hours. If invited to a restaurant, it is a courtesy to leave the ordering of food to your host. If invited to someone's home, take a little present like flowers, or a cake. The different types of eating houses are discussed in Chapter 5.

Visiting the cinema

Greek cinemas show a large number of American and British films, nearly always dubbed with Greek subtitles. Admission is normally around 2,000 GRD depending on location. In summer, a number of cinemas set up for the evening on unused car parks, making the most of the open air.

Enjoying the theatre

Athens alone has some 45 theatres. The ancient theatre of Epidavros is

Key to Codes

1	Class	6	Profession	11	Vat rates
2	Authorisation number	7	Address	12	Unit price
3	Official receipt of retail sale	8	Town	13	Total price
4	Date	9	Quantity	14	Apportionment of VAT
5	Customer	10	Commodity	15	Total payable

Fig. 16. *Loghareeasmó* – a restaurant receipt.

particularly worth visiting. Open air Greek tragedies and comedies are performed during the summer season. These can be well worth a visit for the acoustics and colourful costume.

Visiting museums

There are many major museums primarily in Athens. The National Archaeological museum (*archeologikón mousion*) is the premier museum, which is well worth spending one or two days exploring. The museum is air conditioned (apart from the top floor) and a welcome bolt-hole from the heat of the day. In particular, gold found by the archaeologist Schliemann during his excavations of Mycenae during 1876, thought to be the funeral mask of King Agamemnon, and the 'Jockey of Artemission', a second century BC bronze recovered from the sea after 20 centuries, are definitely worth looking at.

Museum hours
Most museums open at 9.00am on weekdays, 10.00am on Sundays and holidays, and close anywhere from 2.00pm to 7.00pm depending on the season. Archaeological sites usually have somewhat longer hours. In any case it is best to check. All museums and sites close on January 1 and some of the other national holidays. Most museums in Athens are free to enter on Sundays during the winter (to enable all Greeks, whether rich or poor, to learn of their heritage). The Central Archaeological Council has recently announced a sharp increase in the price of admission at the Acropolis, Greece's most popular tourist site. The new price for visitors is 4,000 GRD, doubling the previous ticket cost. Young people under 18 enter without charge and there are reduced rates for senior citizens at most museums and sites. However, the price will include entrance to the Acropolis Museum due to open in time for the Olympic Games in 2004. Many Greeks hope and pray that the new museum will be the final resting place of the *Parthenon Sculptures* (Elgin Marbles).

Viewing the ancient sites

You will soon discover for yourself the many joys of touring the archaeological sites and museums. You could easily spend a memorable fortnight touring from Athens to the Peloponnese taking in the Acropolis, Delphi (the seat of the Oracle), Olympia, Epidavros, Mycenae (tomb of Agamemnon) and the Venetian fortress at Náfplio.

Making your own entertainment

Particularly in Athens, there are a myriad of international singing and amateur dramatic groups, which regularly advertise for new members in the English speaking media (*Athens News, The Hellenic Star, Atlantis*). A few are named below, others are listed in Useful Addresses.

- **HAMS** – The Hellenic Amateur Musical Society meet regularly in Athens and put on two shows per year normally consisting of American musicals, English operettas and pantomimes.

- **English Theatre Club** – a lively group located at 62 Dinocratous Street, Kolonaki, Athens.

- **Athens Singers** – meet regularly to produce concerts of quality music.

GOING TO CHURCH

The orthodox Greek churches are spectacular to visit. Religion is a very important part of the daily diet for Greeks. In Athens, however, there are only three Church of England congregations that meet regularly. Holy Communion and Sunday School are available every Sunday. There are also inter-denominational and Catholic Churches where services are regularly held in English. See Useful Addresses for venues of religious services.

Celebrating the Festivals

One of the loveliest aspects of living in Greece is that a party (*panagiriá*) is never far away. The Greek calendar is filled with religious celebrations largely based on the saints' 'name-sake' days. Festivals on the national holidays are always joyous affairs. In particular, the Feast of Saint Basil on January 1 celebrates the start of the New Year by the baking of a cake *vassilopita* with a coin in it. Whoever finds the coin is wished good luck for the forthcoming year.

ENTERTAINING CHILDREN

The great outdoors life of sand and sea is normally all your children will need, but if you are living in central Athens you may not be able to escape to the beach so easily. Some of the available facilities include:

- **Amusement Parks**. Not very evident in Greece but you can find small concerns with merry-go-rounds *etc*. You are more likely to come across organised playgroups set out in the woods for adventure.

- **Bowling**. An American import, Blands Bowling in Athens has 18 lanes and provides great fun.

- **Greek Folk Art Museum**. English speaking groups can enjoy traditional handicrafts and workshops are regularly arranged.

- **Hellenic Children's Museum**. Courses are run on the local crafts. Trips are organised to other museums e.g. Train Museum and National Archaeological Museum – children's educational leaflets, printed in English, are available.

- **Libraries**. The British Council Library (see Useful Addresses) has lots of children's books, together with a children's reading area. Also, in the corner of the National Garden is a children's library containing almost 100 books in English and French.

- **National History Museum**. The Goulandis Museum, in Kifissia, contains thousands of examples of preserved animal and plant life, fossils and even prehistoric monsters – specially rebuilt!

- **Planetarium**. Although the vocals are in Greek, the visuals and music make this trip very worthwhile, especially as admission is free.

- **Punch and Judy shows**. Theatres regularly put on performances to encourage children to visit.

- **Scouts and Guides**. These international movements are actively promoted in Greece.

- **Skating**. Both ice and roller blading are available.

- **Summer Camps**. An American invention now very popular.

- **Zoos**. There are two or three in Athens, none are really worth visiting.

LEARNING THE LANGUAGE

It is essential that you start to learn the Greek language as best as you are able.

Indeed at the age of 42, Tolstoy is reputed to have begun teaching himself Greek, reasoning that 'without a knowledge of Greek, there is no education'. Not only will the Greeks truly admire you for trying, but also outside Athens and the popular tourist areas you will be lost without it. As you start to pick up words, you will notice that the Greek alphabet, containing only 24 letters as it does, is very different to the Roman alphabet used in English. The simple courtesies mean a lot in Greece. From day one you should work the following polite exchanges into your everyday small talk:

- Please   *Parakaló*
- Thank you   *Efharistó*
- Hello   *Yá sas*
- Welcome   *Hérete*
- Good morning   *Kaliméra*
- Good afternoon   *Kalispéra*
- Good night   *Kalinikta.*

CASE STUDIES

Graham finds Paradise too hot

Graham is aware that nude sunbathing is deeply frowned on by Greeks in general and even forbidden in certain areas. However, he is also aware that the island of Míkanos has a more cavalier and western attitude to this form of bathing than most islands. Asking around, he is directed to the infamous Paradise beach to get his all over tan. Here he joins in the freedom of the movement with almost everyone else sunbathing. That evening, a visit to the local *farmakio* is a clear priority to purchase the most soothing after-sun lotion he can find. The combination of strong midday sun and exposing areas of the anatomy normally covered up leaves Graham badly burnt.

Tony and Wendy go to church

Tony and Wendy are keen to introduce their daughter Abigail to Sunday School while they live in Athens. They visited the British embassy and are introduced to a commercial attaché who tells them of three Church of England congregations they can join locally. They spend the next three Sundays sharing Holy Communion at each church, finally agreeing that All Saints church in nearby Voula suits them best, because the morning service starts at 10.00am every Sunday and Abigail can go to Sunday School at the same time. The Chaplain welcomes them warmly and they are soon accepted into the expatriate community, making lots of friends outside their teaching circle.

John and Betty get searched

After enjoying the Christmas and New Year festivities back home in Derbyshire, John and Betty fly to Athens to stay with friends until Easter. At the airport they are routinely searched and courteously sent on their way with a *Kaló Taxidhi* (have a good journey). Unfortunately, the Dutch couple next to them are not so lucky. The Customs officials find a small quantity of cannabis in the young man's luggage, and they are both promptly marched away. John is informed that drug smuggling, no matter how insignificant an amount, is a very serious matter in Greece due to the growing addiction problems. The official warns John that the punishment for such an offence is up to twelve months' imprisonment, and for more commercial drugs for resale offences, a fine of up to 500,000,000 GRD or even in extreme cases, life imprisonment.

POINTS TO CONSIDER

1. Before choosing a school, have you spent enough time looking at the options, talking with staff, parents and pupils, and really thinking through what kind of education you would like your children to receive?

2. Are you sufficiently extrovert to enjoy the benefits of the many clubs offering sporting facilities, or are you happier doing things on your own? What would the effect on you be of not joining any associations outside your immediate circle of friends?

3. How many cinemas, theatres and museums are near where you live? Have you spent enough time making enquiries to establish what recreational activities are on offer?

Further Reading

ANCIENT HISTORY

Alexander the Great, Robin Lane Fox (Penguin). A serious history study.

Byzantine and Medieval Greece, Churches, Castles and Art, Paul Hetherington (various). Useful introduction to Byzantine and Frankish mainland Greece.

Byzantium: the Early Centuries, John Julius Norwich (Penguin). History of the Byzantine empire.

Democracy and Classical Greece, John Kenyon Davis (Fontana). Account of political growth.

Early Greece, Oswyn Murray (Fontana). Historical account of development from Mycenaeans and Minoans to classical era.

Greece and the Hellenistic World, John Boardman *et al* (Oxford). Fascinating and well illustrated history of the classical world.

The Hellenistic World, F. W. Walbank (Fontana). Historical account of development of Macedonians and Romans.

History of Greece, A. R. Burn (Penguin). General introduction to ancient Greece.

Medieval Greece, Nicholas Cheetham (Yale). Historical study of Byzantine and Ottoman eras.

The Orthodox Church, Timothy Callistos Ware (Penguin). Introduction to the established religion of Greece.

The World of Odysseus, M. I. Finley (Penguin). Detailed account of Mycenaean myth and fact.

ARCHAEOLOGY AND ART

The Aegean Civilizations, Peter Warren (Phaidon). Illustrated account of the Minoan and Mycenaean cultures.

The Arts in Prehistoric Greece, Sinclair Hood (Penguin). Lovely introduction to the early art.

Classical Greece, Roger Ling (Phaidon). Illustrated account of art in classical Greece.

The Cycladic Spirit, Colin Renfrew (Thames & Hudson). Study of Cycladic artefacts.

Early Christian and Byzantine Art, John Beckwith (Penguin). Illustrated study introducing Byzantine art.

The Elgin Marbles, B. F. Cook (British Museum). Well illustrated account of the history of the Parthenon Sculptures.

Greek Art, John Boardman (Thames & Hudson). Good introduction to Greek art.

Greek Style, Suzanne Slesin & Co (Thames & Hudson). Visual collection of interiors from various islands.

A Guide to the History and Myth of 15 Selected Sites in Southern Greece, Alan Carter (Efstathidadis). Background reading on remains of 15 archaeological sites.

A Handbook of Greek Art, Gisela Richter (Phaidon). Survey of the visual arts of ancient Greece.

Hellenistic Sculpture, R. R. R. Smith (Thames & Hudson). Modern look at art of Greece during reign of Alexander the Great.

The King Must Die, The Last of the Wine, The Mask of Opollo, Mary Renault (Sceptre). Wonderful myths of early Greeks.

Minoan and Mycenaean Art, Reynold Higgins (Thames & Hudson). Well illustrated introduction to the art of the day.

Road to Rembetika, Gail Holst (Denise Harvey). Excellent introduction to the music, people and culture of Rembetika.

BUSINESS AND LAW

Barclays Business Guide to Greece, Barclays Bank PLC.

Doing Business in Greece, Ernst & Young. Overview of business practice in Greece, Athens.

Doing Business in Greece, Grant Thornton, Athens.

Greece: A Guide for Businessmen and Investors, Coopers & Lybrand, Athens.

Investment Guide, Hellenic Industrial Development Bank S.A, Athens.

Investment in Greece, KPMG Athens.

Quick Guide to Taxation in Greece, Deloitte & Touche, Athens.

Who Owns Whom is a reference book that can provide the names of British companies with subsidiaries in Greece.

CLASSICS

The Age of Alexander, Plutarch (Penguin).

The Guide to Greece (2 volumes), Pausanias (Penguin).

The Histories, Herodotus (Penguin).
The History of My Times, Xenophon (Penguin).
History of the Peloponnesian War, Thucydides (Penguin).
The Iliad, Homer (Penguin).
The Odyssey, Homer (Penguin).
Plutarch on Sparta, Plutarch (Penguin).
The Rise and Fall of Athens, Plutarch (Penguin).

LIVING AND WORKING

The Au Pair and Nanny's Guide to Working Abroad, Susan Griffiths & Sharon Legg (Vacation Work). Live and work with a family abroad.

Buying a Property Abroad, Niki Chesworth (Kogan Page). Practical guide for overseas homebuyers with a section on Greece.

Catering Careers Abroad, (Eurochef Ltd).

Colloquial Greek, Niki Watts (Routledge). Basic Greek language course.

Directory of Greek Language Courses, (Greek Institute, London). A useful booklet of Greek courses offered by adult education centres, colleges and universities around UK.

The Directory of Jobs & Careers Abroad, André De Vries (Vacation Work).

Europe – A Manual for Hitch-Hikers, (Vacation Work).

Directory of Summer Jobs Abroad, (Vacation Work). Jobs in over 45 countries including Greece.

Guide to Living Abroad, Michael Furnell & Philip Jones (Kogan Page). Financial advice for British expatriates.

How To Get A Job In Europe, Mark Hempshell (How To Books). Useful general review with six pages on Greece.

How to Retire Abroad, Roger Jones (How To Books).

The International Directory of Voluntary Work, David Woodworth (Vacation Work).

Nexus, published by Expatriates Network, is a monthly magazine especially relevant to engineers. Subscription only: PO Box 380, Croydon CR9 2ZQ. Tel: (0044) 020 8 760 5100.

Notes on Greece for British Passport Holders, (British Embassy, Athens).

Overseas Jobs Express is a fortnightly newspaper with advice, reports and advertised vacancies. Subscription only: PO Box 22, Brighton BN1 6HT. Tel: (0127) 344 0220.

A Taste of the Aegean, Andy and Terry Harris (Pavilion). Greek cooking and culture.

Teaching English Abroad, Susan Griffiths (Vacation Work).

The UK Guide to Living and Working in the EC, Miranda Davies (Livewire). Authoritative book on practicalities.

Willings Press Guide, (Reed Information Service). Gives full details of newspapers, consumer and trade journals and periodicals throughout the UK and overseas. It should be available for reference in most public libraries.

Working Abroad: Essential Financial Planning for Expatriates and their Employees, Jonathan Golding (International Venture Handbooks).

Working Holidays, (Central Bureau for Educational Visits and Exchanges).

Working in Greece, (Employment Services Overseas Placing Unit, Sheffield).

Work Your Way Around the World, Susan Griffith (Vacation Work). A practical guide packed with handy hints to getting work abroad including a section on Greece.

Xenophobes Guide to the Greeks, Alexandra Fiada (Ravette). An irreverent look at the beliefs and foibles of the Greeks.

MODERN GREEK FICTION

Captain Corelli's Mandolin, Louis de Bernières (Secker & Warburg). Novel set on Keffalonia during Second World War occupation.

Dowry of Danger, R. L. Smithson (Efstathiadis). Novel based in period of Greek Civil War.

It Begins But Never Ends, Sandra Rogers (Minerva). Novel based around a restaurant bar in Santorini.

The Kalanissos Contract, Ken Pearmain (Citron Press). Mystery story set on the island of Kalanissos.

The Magus, John Fowles (Picador). Mystery novel set on island of Spétses in the 1950s.

Loukas Laras, Demetrios Vikelas (Doric Publications). Nineteenth century novel set on the island of Hios.

The Murderess, Alexandros Papadiamantis (Writers & Readers). Novel set at the turn of the century on Skíathos.

Prospero's Cell, Lawrence Durrell (Faber & Faber).

Zorba the Greek, Nikos Kazantzakis (Faber & Faber). Famous tale by the Cretan master.

MODERN HISTORY

Captain Corelli's Island. Andy and Terry Harris. Ancient and modern history of Keffalonia.

A Concise History of Greece, Richard Clogg (Cambridge). Account of decline of Byzantine empire to modern day.

Farewell Anatolia, Dido Sotiriou (Kedros). Events leading up to the Greek/Turkish exchange of populations in 1922.

The Greeks: The Land and People Since the War, James Pettifer (Viking). A general contemporary look at the country, its people and politics.

Hellas – A Portrait of Greece, Nicholas Gage (Efsthathiadís). A wonderful reflection on the author's love affair with Greece.

Ionian Vision: Greece in Asia Minor (1919-22), Michael Llewellyn Smith (St Martins Press). Account of the Anatolian campaign and war between Greece and Turkey.

Inside Hitler's Greece: The Experience of Occupation (1941-44), Mark Mazower (Yale). Chronicles the events leading up to the civil war.

Modern Greece: A Short Story, C. M. Woodhouse (Faber & Faber). Accurate account of the development of Greece.

Patriots and Scoundrels, John Ponder (Hyland House). Painful but true life story of resistance fighting in the mountains of Central Greece during 1943.

A Traveller's History of Greece, Timothy Boatswain and Colin Nicholson (Windrush Press). Guide through the ages of the history of Greece.

NATURAL HISTORY

Greek Wild Flowers and Plant Life in Ancient Greece, Hellmut Banman *et al*. Illustrated colour guide to wild flowers and shrubs known over the ages.

Medicinal Plants of Greece, George Sfikas (Efsthathiadís). A most informative little handbook.

Trees and Shrubs of Greece, George Sfikis (Efsthathiadís). A useful listing.

Wild Flowers of Crete, George Sfikas (Efstathiadis). An excellent set of photographs.

Wild Flowers of Greece, George Sfikas (Efstathiadís). A comprehensive collection of the best seen flowers.

OLDER GREEK FICTION

The Cyclades, or Life Among Insular Greeks, James Theodore Bent. Published in 1881 the book charts a year's travels in the Aegean.

Greece: A Literary Companion, Martin Garrett (John Murray). A wandering general account of travel in Greece.

In Greece with Pen and Palette, Z C Boyaaijian (J. M. Dent). 1938 travel account.

Legends of Greece and Rome, G H Kupfer (Harrap). Favourite Greek myths.

Short History of Greece, W. S. Robinson (Rivingtons). Summary of Greek history for younger readers written at the turn of the century.

The Song of Troy, Colleen McCullogh (Orion Books). A well written account of the immortal lovers, Helen and Paris.

TRAVEL GUIDES

Baedeker's Greece, (Automobile Association).

Eperons Guide to the Greek Islands, Arthur Eperon (Pan). Wonderful travellers' review of 55 Greek islands.

Fodors Guide to Greece, Various (Fodors Travel Publications). Masterful review of the country and its islands, updated regularly.

Greece by Rail, Zane Katsikis (Bradt). Travelling Greece by rail and ferry.

Greek Island Hopping, Frewin Poffley (Thomas Cook). User friendly guide to ferry network.

Greek Island Hopping 2000 – the Island Hopper's Bible!, (Thomas Cook Publishing).

Greece: Off the Beaten Track, Marc Dubin (Moorland).

In the Footsteps of Lawrence Durrell and Gerald Durrell in Corfu (1934–39), Hilary Whitton Paipeti. Pocket companion to the Corfu works of the Durrell brothers.

The Mountains of Greece – A Walkers Guide, Tim Salmon (Cicerone Press).

The Rough Guide to Crete, John Fisher (Penguin). Practical guide to Crete.

Rough Guide to the Greek Islands, Mark Ellingham & Co (Penguin). Excellent and practical travellers' guide to most of the inhabited islands.

Trekking in Greece, Marc Dubin (Lonely Planet). Excellent walker's guide for day hikes and longer treks.

Visitors Guide to Athens and Peloponnese, Brian and Eileen Anderson (Moorland). Detailed travellers' guide of the area.

Which Guide to Greece and The Greek Islands (Penguin). Good overall review.

TRAVEL WRITING

An Affair of the Heart, Dilys Powell (Hodder and Stoughton). Enormously readable account of three visits to Greece in 1940s/50s.

A Bottle in the Shade, Peter Levi (Sinclair–Stevenson). A journey in the Western Peloponnese.

The Colossus of Maroussi, Henry Miller (Minerva). A picture of Corfu in 1939.

The Corfu Years, Edward Lear (Denise Harvey, Athens). Illustrated journals by the famous landscape painter.

The Cretan Journal, Edward Lear (Denise Harvey, Athens). Illustrated journals by the famous landscape painter.

Dinner with Persephone, Patricia Storace (Granta). Travels around Greece 1994/95.

Flight of Ikaros, Kevin Andrews. Thrilling account of travel in the Greek countryside during the civil war following the Second World War.

Journey to the Gods, John Hillaby (Constable). Backpacking through the Pindos mountains.

Lugworm Homeward Bound, Ken Duxbury (Pelham). Greece to England in an open dingy.

Mani – Travels in the Southern Peloponnese, Patrick Leigh Fermour (Penguin). Travels through Greece by the famous Cretan war resistance fighter.

Roumeli, Patrick Leigh Fermour (Penguin). Travels through Greece by the famous Cretan war resistance fighter.

Unearthing Atlantis, Charles Pellegrino (various). Excellent account of Santorini.

The Unwritten Places, Tim Salmon (Lycabettus). Travel account of Agrapha in the Pindos mountains.

TRUE LIFE EXPERIENCES

An Island Apart, Sarah Wheeler (Abacus). Detailed five-month diary on a remote island – Evvia.

Attic in Greece, Austen Kark (Little Brown & Co). House restoration in Nápflio.

Bitter Lemons, Lawrence Durrell (Faber & Faber).

The Cretan Runner, George Psychoundakis (John Murray). Invasion of Crete translated by Patrick Leigh-Fermour.

Ela – A Greek Affair, Michael Saunders (Efsthathiadís). Amusing account of buying a house in a Cretan mountain village.

Eleni, Nicholas Gage (Harper Collins). Powerful story of the tragic events that took place to the author's mother in a small village during the Civil War.

The Hill of Kronos, Peter Levi (Harvill). A personal portrait of Greece.

The History of a Vendetta, Yioros Yatromanolakis (Dedalus). Tales of two families involved in murder on Crete.

The House by the Sea, Rebecca Camhi Fromer (Mercury House). The holocaust that almost wiped out the Jewish community of Thessaloniki.

Intermezzo in Atlantis, Elizabeth Karlhuber (Efstathiadís). A lovely story which will touch the heart of anyone having visited Santorini.

The Last Lemon Grove, Jackson Webb (Weidenfeld). An American's view of life in a remote village on Crete.

Life in the Tomb, Stratis Myrivilis (Quartet). War memoirs from the Macedonian front of 1917–18.

Lizzie's Paradise, Elizabeth Parker (Mellina–Verlag). True story of taking over a run-down yacht club on the tiny island of Trizonia.

My Family and Other Animals, Gerald Durrell (Penguin). Durrell's childhood on Corfu.

Officers and Gentlemen, Evelyn Waugh (Penguin). Well written account of the battle of Crete and its subsequent evacuation.

The Olive Grove – Travels in Greece, Katherine Kizilos (Lonely Planet). Glimpses into the life of a Greek family in the Northern Peloponnese.

On a Greek Island, Fionnula Brennan (Poolbeg Press Ltd). Buying a house and living on Paros.

A Place for Us, Nicholas Gage (Black Swan). Continues the story of Eleni's children – a tale of success and family pride.

Portrait of a Greek Mountain Village, Juliet Du Boulay (Oxford UP). A 1960s account of life on Évvia.

Portrait of Greece, Nicholas Gage. (Efstathiadís Group). Beautiful and descriptive introduction to Greece.

Reflections on a Marine Venus, Lawrence Durrell (Faber & Faber). Wartime experiences and impressions of Rhodes.

Seduced by a Greek Island and Aegean Summer, Mimi La Follete Summerskill (Efsthathiadís). Building a house on the island of Ios.

The Seventh Garment, Eugenia Fakinou (Serpents Tail). Life stories of three generations of women from the War of Independence to military junta.

Vanishing Greece, Clay Perry (Abbeville Press). Pictures of a way of life in rural Greece.

Useful Addresses

ACCOUNTANCY FIRMS

Deloitte & Touche, 250-254 Kifissias Avenue, 152 31 Halandri, Athens. Tel: (01) 677 6600.

Ernst & Young, 3–5 Ilission Street, 115 28 Athens. Tel: (01) 772 7000.

KPMG Kyriacou, 3 Stratigou Tombra Street, Aghia Paraskevi, 153 42 Athens. Tel: (01) 60 62 100.

Moore Stephens SA, 93 Akti Miaouli, 185 38 Piraeus. Tel: (01) 429 0620.

Price Waterhouse Coopers SA, 47 Vas Erakliou Street, 54623 Thessaloniki. Tel: (031) 268 921.

Price Waterhouse Coopers SA, 268 Kifisias Avenue, Halandri, 152 32 Athens. Tel: (01) 687 4400.

ALIENS BUREAU OFFICES

173 Alexandra Avenue, Athens. Tel: (01) 641 1746.

14 Athanassiou Diakou Street, Pallini, Athens. Tel: (01) 603 2980.

3 Damoukara Street, Lavrio, Athens. Tel: (02) 922 5265.

18 Iroon Polytechniou Street, Elefsina, Athens. Tel: (01) 554 7427.

37 Iroon Polytechniou Street, Piraeus, Athens. Tel: (01) 412 4133.

23 Karaiskaki Street, Glyfada, Athens. Tel: (01) 962 7068.

BRITISH EMBASSIES AND CONSULATES

British Council, Platia Philikis, Etairias 17, Post Box 3488, Kolonaki Square, 10 210 Athens. Tel: (01) 369 2333.

British Embassy, 1 Ploutarchou Street, 10 675 Athens. Tel (01) 723 6211.

Consulate, 2 Alexandras Avenue, 491 00 Corfu. Tel: (0661) 30055.

Consulate, 3 Pavlou Mela Street, Rhodes 851 00. Tel: (0241) 27247.

Consulate, 8 Venizelou Street, Eleftherias Square, 546 24 Thessaloniki. Tel: (031) 278006.

Vice Consulate, 8 Akti Petrou Ralli, Ermoupolis, 841 00 Syros. Tel: (0281) 22232.

Vice Consulate, 5 Foskolos Street, 291 00 Zakynthos. Tel: (0695) 48030.

Vice Consulate, 8 Laoumitzi Annetas Street, 853 00 Kos. Tel: (0242) 26203.

Vice Consulate, 16 Papalexandrou Street, 712 02 Heraklion, Crete. Tel: (081) 224012.

Vice Consulate, 45 Thessaloniki Street, Kavala. Tel: (051) 223704.

Vice Consulate, 2 Votsi Street, 262 21 Patras. Tel: (061) 277329.

CHAMBERS OF COMMERCE

Athens Chamber of Commerce and Industry, 7 Akadimias Street, 10671 Athens. Tel: (01) 360 4815.

British Hellenic Chamber of Commerce, Northern Greece Office, 47 Vas Irakliou Street, 54624 Thessaloniki. Tel: (031) 268 515.

British Hellenic Chamber of Commerce, 25 Vas Sofias Avenue, 10674 Athens. Tel: (01) 721 0361.

Economic Chamber of Greece, 6 Aristidou Street, 10556 Athens. Tel: (01) 323 3967.

International Chamber of Commerce, 27 Kaningos Street, 10682 Athens. Tel: (01) 361 0879.

Piraeus Chamber of Commerce and Industry, 1 Londovikou Street, 18531 Piraeus. Tel: (01) 417 7241.

CUSTOMS OFFICES

Athens Airport Customs Office, 16603 Elliniko, Athens. Tel: (01) 962 3261.

Athens Customs Office, Stathmos Larissis, 10000 Athens. Tel: (01) 513 1591.

Directorate for the Supervision & Control of Cars, DIPEAK, 32 Akti Kondyli, 185 10 Piraeus. Tel: (01) 462 3615.

Director of Customs, Ministry of Finance, 10 Karageorgi Servias Street, 10184 Athens. Tel: (01) 347 8706.

Piraeus Customs Office, Agiou Nikolaou Square, 18500 Piraeus. Tel: (01) 451 1003.

EDUCATION OFFICES

Certification Unit, The British Chambers of Commerce, Westwood House, Westwood Business Park, Coventry CV4 8HS.

Comparability Co-ordinator, Dr N Iliadis, Paidagogiko Institouto, Messogian Avenue 396, 15341 Athens.

Comparability Co-ordinator Employment Department, Qualifications and Standards Branch QSI, Room E454, Moorfoot, Sheffield S1 4PQ. Tel: (0114) 259 4144.

Comparability Co-ordinator, Mmes A Georgiadou/E Constanta-copoulou, Ypourgio Pedias & Politismou, Metropoleos Street, 10185 Athens.

Dikatsa, Syngrou Avenue 112, 11741 Athens. Tel: (01) 922 2533.

European Council for International Schools, 21B Lavant Street, Petersfield, Hants GU32 3EL. Tel: (01730) 68244.

General Education Directorate, Ministry of Education, 15 Metropoleos Street, 10557 Athens. Tel: (01) 323 0461.

Greek Embassy, Education Office, 1A Holland Park, London W11 3TP. Tel: (020) 7221 5977.

The Greek Institute, 34 Bush Hill Road, London N21 2DS. Tel: (020) 8360 7968.

Ministry of Education & Culture, Ypourgio Pedias & Politismou, Metropoleos Street 15, 10185 Athens. Tel: (01) 323 0461.

National Academic Recognition Information Centre (NARIC), DIKATSA, 112 Leoforos Syngrou, 11741 Athens. Tel: (01) 921 8052.

Network Educational Services, 31 Vournazou Street, 11521 Athens. Tel: (01) 645 3051.

Society for the Promotion of Hellenic Studies (The Hellenic Society), Senate House, Malet Street, London WC1E 7HU. Tel: (020) 7862 8730.

Unecia, Universities of England Consortium for International Activities, PO Box 51162, 14510 Athens. Tel: (01) 612 3139.

EMPLOYMENT SERVICES

Centre for Occupational Health & Safety, 6 Dodekanissou Street, 17456 Alimos, Athens. Tel: (01) 999 9566.

CEPEC Recruitment Guide, 67 Jermyn Street, London SW1Y 6NY. Tel: (020) 7930 0322.

Department of Social Security, Overseas Advice Department, Hannibal

House, London SE1 6LZ. Tel: (020)7 210 3000.

Department of Social Security, Overseas Branch, Benton Park Road, Newcastle upon Tyne NE98 1YX. Tel: (0191) 213 5000.

Employment Service, Overseas Placing Unit, Rockingham House, 123 West Street, Sheffield, S1 4ER.

Executive Services Limited, Athens Tower, Building B Suite 506, 2 Messogian Street, 11527 Athens. Tel: (01) 778 3698.

Federation of Greek Industries, 5 Xenofontos Street, 10557 Athens. Tel: (01) 323 7325.

Greek Personnel Management Association, 3 Karitsi Street, G-10561 Athens. Tel: (01) 322 5704.

Link Resources International, 36 Voulis Street, 10557 Athens. Tel: (01) 322 2858.

Ministry of Labour, 40 Piraeus Street, Athens. Tel: (01) 523 2110.

Ministry of Labour, Ypourgio Ergassias, Tmima Diethon Scheseon, Piraeus Street 40, 10182 Athens. Tel: (01) 522 9140.

OAED, EURES (SEDOC), Ethnikis Antistasis 8, 16610 A. Kalamaki, Athens. Tel: (01) 994 2466.

OAED (Manpower & Job Placement Agency), Thrakis 8, 16610 Glyfada, Athens. Tel: (01) 993 2589.

REC, 36–38 Mortimer Street, London W1N 7RB. Tel: 0800 320588.

ENGLISH LANGUAGE SCHOOLS AND UNIVERSITIES

American College of Greece, Gravias Street, Agia Paraskavi, 15300 Athens. (Useful address for penfriends.)

American Community Schools of Athens, Halandri Campus, 129 Aghias Paraskevis Street, Ani Halandri, 15234 Athens. Tel: (01) 639 3200.

Athens College, Psychico, 15400 Athens.

Athens New York College, 38 Amalias Street, 10558 Athens. Tel: (01) 322 5961.

BCA Business Studies, 4 Dimitressa Street, 11528 Athens. Tel: (01) 725 3783.

Byron College, Athens, 7 Filolaou Street, Gargitos, Geraka, 153 44 Athens. Tel: (01) 604 7722.

Campion Junior School, 114 Aghias Paraskevis Street, Halandri, Athens. Tel: (01) 682 3134. (Relocating late 2000.)

Campion Senior School, Dimitros and Antheon Street, Ekali, Athens. Tel: (01) 813 3883. (Relocating late 2000.)

Central Bureau for Educational Visits & Exchanges, 10 Spring Gardens, London SW1A 2BN. Tel: (020) 7389 4004.

Green Hill International School,18 Venezuelas Street, Ano Glyfada, 166 74 Athens. Tel: (01) 964 1782.

ICBS Thessaloníkí Business School, PO Box 46, Oreokastro, 57013 Thessaloníkí. Tel: (031) 698 598.

Mediterranean College, 18 Omonia Square, 10431 Athens. Tel: (01) 325 0826.

Peter Pan Nursery School, 4-6 Lakonias Street, Athens. Tel: (01) 895 9654.

The Old Mill, Kolokotroni 21, Kefalari, Kifissia, Athens. Tel: (01) 801 2558.

St Catherine's British Embassy Primary School, Kondoyanni and El Venizelou Streets, Lykovryssi, Kifissia, Athens. Tel: (01) 2829 750.

St Lawrence College, 2 Delta Street, Hellenikon, 16777 Athens. Tel: (01) 894 4602 (senior) (01) 894 0696 (junior) (due to relocate in 2002).

Studies of Business Science (SBS), 57 Panepistimious Street, 10664 Athens. Tel: (01) 324 2900.

Tasis Hellenic International School, PO Box 51025, 14510 Kifissia, Athens. Tel: (01) 801 1426.

University of Indianapolis, 29 Vaulis Street, Syntagma Square, 10557 Athens. Tel: (01) 323 6647.

ENGLISH SPEAKING CLUBS AND SOCIETIES

American Society of Greece. 500-member society meeting weekly. Tel: (01) 672 5485.

American Women's Organisation of Greece. Tel: (01) 362 4115.

Athenians Hockey Club. Tel: (01) 813 1767.

Athens Hash House Harriers and the Full Moon Hash. Social jogging groups with 80 members meeting weekly. Tel: (01) 801 0861.

Athens Hockey Club. Tel: (01) 813 1767.

Athens International Nurses Association. Tel: (01) 988 0111.

Athens Singers. Tel: (01) 691 2314.

Athens Spartans Rugby Club. Tel: (01) 429 3271.

Greek–Irish Society. Tel: (01) 600 1355.

Hellenic Amateur Musical Society. Tel: (01) 691 2314.

Hellenic–American Union. Educational seminars and cultural events. Tel: (01) 362 9886.

Link-Up. English-speakers social gatherings with over 300 members. Tel: (01) 923 1171.

Newcomers. Welcomes members newly arrived in Athens. Tel: (01) 808 7017.

North Athens Singles and Divorced Club. Tel: (01) 672 5485.

FINANCIAL INSTITUTIONS

Abbey National Building Society, Overseas Mortgages Dept, Abbey House, Baker Street, London NW1 6XL. Tel: (020) 7612 4000.

Athens Stock Exchange, 10 Sophocleous Street, 10 559 Athens. Tel: (01) 321 1301.

Barclays Country Reports, Librarian, Economics Department, Barclays Bank plc, PO Box 12, 1 Wimborne Road, Poole, Dorset BH15 2BB. Tel: (01202) 671212.

Bennet & Co, International Lawyers, 39 London Road, Alderley Edge, Cheshire SK9 7JY. Tel: (01625) 586937.

Blackstone Franks, Overseas Taxation Planning Dept, Barbican House, 26-34 Old Street, London EC1 9HL. Tel: (020) 7250 3300.

Dobson & Sinisi, International Lawyers, Kanari 7, 10671 Athens. Tel: (01) 364 2320.

DTI - Greece Desk, Room 850, Kingsgate House, 66-74 Victoria Street, London W1E 6SW. Tel: (020) 7215 5000.

Emborika & Viomichaniko Epimelitino Athinon (EBEA), Akadimias 7-9, 10671 Athens. Tel: (01) 362 2157 (for information on Greek companies).

Export Promotion Council, 24 Stadiou Street, 10564 Athens. Tel: (01) 322 6875.

Federation of Greek Industries, 5 Xenofontos Street, 105 57 Athens. Tel: (01) 323 7325.

ICAP A.E. 64 Vas. Sophias, 115 28 Athens. Tel: (01) 725 0601.

National Statistical Organisation, 14-16 Lykourgou Street, 10166 Athens. Tel: (01) 328 9396.

FOREIGN BANKS IN GREECE

ABN Amro Bank, 330 Thisseos Avenue, PO Box 78540. Kallithea, 17675 Athens. Tel: (01) 949 7199.

ANZ Grindlays Bank plc, 7 Merlin Street, 10671 Athens. Tel: (01) 362 4601.

Bank of America, N.A., 35 Panepistimiou Street, 10564 Athens. Tel: (01) 325 1901.

Bank of Nova Scotia (The), 37 Panepistimiou Street, 10564 Athens. Tel: (01) 361 4810.

Barclays Bank plc, 15 Voukourestiou Street, 10671 Athens. Tel: (01) 364 4311.

Barclays Bank plc, 1 Kolokotroni Street 10562 Athens. Tel: (01) 331 0580.

Citibank N.A., 8 Othonos Street 10557 Athens. Tel: (01) 322 7471.

Coutts Bank (Switzerland) Ltd, 19 Voukourestiou Street, 10671 Athens. Tel: (01) 363 5430.

HSBC Plc, 1A Sekeri Street, 10671 Athens. Tel: (01) 364 7410.

HSBC Plc, 93 Akti Miaouli Street, 18538 Piraeus. Tel: (01) 429 0120/4.

HSBC Plc (Salonika), 4 I. Dragoumi Street, 54624 Thessaloniki. Tel: (031) 267014/270948.

National Westminster Bank plc, 5 Korai Street, 10564 Athens. Tel: (01) 324 1562.

National Westminster Bank plc, 7 II Merarchias Street, 18535 Piraeus. Tel: (01) 411 7415.

National Westminster Bank plc, 3 I. Dragoumi Street, 54625 Thessaloniki. Tel: (031) 531007.

Royal Bank of Scotland plc, 61 Akti Miaouli, 18510 Piraeus. Tel: (01) 459 6500.

Thomas Cook Foreign Money Limited, 4 Karageorgi Servias Street, 10562 Athens. Tel: (01) 322 0155.

FOREIGN INSURANCE COMPANIES

ACE Hellas, Commerical Centre Office 114, 85 Vouliagmenis Avenue, P.O. Box 70287, Glyfada 16674, Athens. Tel: (01) 964 9683.

Bary S.A. – Avon Insurance Plc, 26 Akadimias, 10671 Athens. Tel: (01) 360 7808.

CGU Insurance, 91 Mihalakopoulou Street, 11528 Athens. Tel: (01) 772 8800.

Ecclesiastical Insurance Office Plc, 5 Stadiou Street, 10562 Athens. Tel: (01) 322 7357.

InterAmerican Group of Companies, 117 Kifissias Avenue, 151 80 Maroussi, Athens. Tel: (01) 619 1222.

Metrolife Insurance Co. SA, 213–215 Syngrou Avenue, Nea Smyrni, 17121 Athens. Tel: (01) 937 0120.

Willis Corroon Hellas SA, 44 Ermou Street, 10563 Athens. Tel: (01) 322 9601/3.

GREEK BANKS

Alpha Credit Bank A E, 40 Stadiou Street, 10252 Athens. Tel: (01) 326 0000.

Bank of Greece, 21 Panepistimiou Street, 10564 Athens. Tel: (01) 320 1111.

Commercial Bank S.A., 11 Sophocleous Street, 10235 Athens. Tel: (01) 328 4000.

General Hellenic Bank SA, 9 Panepistimiou Street, 10229 Athens. Tel: (01) 327 7000.

Hellenic Industrial Development Bank SA (ETBA), 87 Syngrou Avenue, 11745 Athens. Tel: (01) 924 2900.

Ionian Bank, 45 Panepistimiou Street, 10243 Athens. Tel: (01) 322 5501.

Macedonia Thrace Bank, 5 Ionos Dragoumi Street, 54625 Thessaloniki. Tel: (031) 542 2213.

National Bank of Greece, 50 St Mary Axe, London EC3A 8EL. Tel: (020) 7626 3222.

National Bank of Greece, 86 Eolou Street, 10232 Athens. Tel: (01) 334 1000.

Piraeus Bank S.A., 5 Souri Street & Amalias Av, 10557 Athens. Tel: (01) 333 5000.

GREEK EMBASSIES, CONSULATES AND VICE CONSULATES IN THE UK

2A Coates Crescent, Edinburgh EH3 7AL. Tel: (0131) 225 6744.

41 Archers Road, Southampton SO1 2NF. Tel: (01703) 225585.

98 Baronald Drive, Glasgow G12 0HY. Tel: (0141) 334 0360.

Greek Embassy, 1A Holland Park, London W11 3TP. Tel: (020) 7221 6467.

Hagley Court, 229 Hagley Road, Birmingham B16 9RP. Tel: (0121) 454 3369.

Hurst House, 15-19 Corporation Square, Belfast BT1 3AJ. Tel: (01232) 242242.

'Melathron', 8 Foxhill Drive, Leeds LS16 5PG. Tel: (0113) 278 3123.

INTERNATIONAL BOOKSELLERS

Compendium Bookshop, 28 Nikis Street, Athens.

Educational Books, 14 Niridon Street, Athens. Tel: (01) 723 9474.

Efsthathiadis Group, 84 Academias Street, 10678 Athens. Tel: (01) 383 7439.

Eleftheroudakis, 17 Panepistimiou Street, Athens. Tel: (01) 331 4180.

Evripidis, 11 Vas Konstantinou, Halandri, Nr Athens. Tel: (01) 680 0644.

Gazelle Book Services (UK distributors for Efsthathiades), Falcon House, Queen Square, Lancaster LA1 1RN. Tel: (01524) 68765.

Hellenic Book Service, 91 Fortess Road, London NW5 1AG. Tel: (020) 7267 9499.

Kakoulidis Book Store, 25–29 Panepistimiou Street, Athens.

Leader Books, 45 Benaki Street, Athens. Tel: (01) 381 1937.

Publicitas Ltd, 525 Fulham Road, London SW6. Tel: (020) 7385 7723.

Stanfords, 12–14 Long Acre, London WC2E 9LP. Tel: (020) 7836 1321.

The Travellers Bookshop, 25 Cecil Court, London WC2N 4EX. Tel: (020) 7836 9132.

Xenos Booksellers, 6 Denmark Street, London WC2. Tel: (020) 7240 1968.

Zambox, 5 Mavrokordatou, Athens. Tel: (01) 382 3564.

MARINE CONTACTS

Lloyds Register of Shipping, 87 Atki Miaouli, 4th Floor, 18538 Piraeus. Tel: (01) 429 1051.

Overseas Maritime Consultants EPE, 72 Kolokotrini Street, 18535 Piraeus. Tel: (01) 422 2730–6.

Salvage Association, Xylas House, Akti Miaouli & Filellion 1–3, 18536 Piraeus. Tel: (01) 429 360.

Small Ships Register, DVLA, Swansea SA99 1BX. Tel: (01792) 783355.

West of England (Hellas) Ltd, 26 Skouse Street, 18536 Piraeus. Tel: (01) 453 1969.

MEDICAL ORGANISATIONS

Association of Graduate Nurses, Athens Tower, Building C, 2nd Floor, 2 Messogion Avenue, 11527 Athens. Tel: (01) 770 2861.

BUPA International, Equity & Law House, 102 Queens Road, Brighton BN1 3XT. Tel: (01273) 608 1212.

BUPA International, European Medical Services, 240 Syngrou Avenue, 17672 Kallithea, Athens. Tel: (01) 957 6256.

Chest X Rays & Blood Tests: Evangelismos Hospital, Outpatients Department, Athens. Tel: (01) 7200 001.

Department of Health, Overseas Advice Dept, PO Box 21, Stanmore, Middlesex HA7 1AY. Tel: (020) 7210 4850.

Drug Tracing: General State Hospital, Toxicological Laboratory, Messogion Avenue, Athens. Tel: (01) 7706 301.

Idrima Kinonikon Afaliseon (IKA), 64 Pireous Street, 10436 Athens.

International Relations Office (IKA), Tmima Diethon Scheseon, 178 Kifissias Avenue, 15231 Athens. Tel: (01) 647 1140.

Private Patients Plan, PPP House, Upperton Road, Eastbourne, Sussex BN21 1LH. Tel: (01323) 410505.

Psychiatric Evaluation: General Mental Hospital, Outpatients Department, 17 Psaron Street, Athens. Tel: (01) 5232 359.

Social Insurance Foundation (Idrima Kinonikon Asfaliseon — IKA), 64 Pireos Street, 10436 Athens.

WPA Health Insurance, Rivergate House, Blackbrook Park, Taunton, Somerset TA1 2PE. Tel: (01823) 623330.

MINISTRIES

British Council Reading Room, Filikis Etairias 17, Kolonaki Square, 10673 Athens. Tel: (01) 363 3211.

Ministry of Agriculture, Fisheries & Food, Government Buildings, Hook Rise South, Polworth, Surbiton, Surrey KT6 7NF. Tel: (020) 8330 4411.

Ministry of Commerce (International Trade), Kaningos Square, 10677 Athens. Tel: (01) 381 6241.

Ministry of Development Building, 5th Floor, Canninges Square, 10681 Athens. Tel: (01) 382 9411.

Ministry of Education & Religion, Ypourigo Pedias & Politsmou, 15 Metropoleos Street, 10185 Athens. Tel: (01) 323 0461.

Ministry of Energy and National Resources, 80 Michalakopoulou Street, 11528 Athens. Tel: (01) 770 8615.

Ministry of the Environment, Regional Planning and Public Works, 2 Harilaou Trikoipi Street, 10178 Athens. Tel: (01) 644 9113.

Ministry of Finance, 10 Karageorgi Servias Street, 10184 Athens. Tel: (01) 322 4071.

Ministry of Foreign Affairs, 1 Akadimias, 10671 Athens. Tel: (01) 361 0581.

Ministry of Justice, 96 Messogion Avenue, 11526 Athens. Tel: (01) 777 1871.

Ministry of Labour, 40 Pireos Street, 10182 Athens. Tel: (01) 523 3111.

Ministry of Merchant Marine, 150 G. Lambraki, 18535 Piraeus. Tel: (01) 412 1211.

Ministry of National Economy, 1 Syntagma Square, 10180 Athens. Tel: (01) 323 0931.

Ministry of National Economy, Dept for Attracting Investments, 1 Syntagma Square, 10180 Athens. Tel: (01) 324 6425.

Ministry of National Economy, Private Investment Policy Division, 42 Akadimis Street, 10672 Athens. Tel: (01) 364 7874.

Ministry of Public Order (Public Relations Department), Kafelaki 1, 11525 Athens. Tel: (01) 692 8510.

Ministry of Transport and Communications, 13 Xenofontos Street, 10191 Athens. Tel: (01) 325 121119.

MOTORING AND CAR HIRE ORGANISATIONS

Automobile Association, Fanum House, PO Box 51, Basingstoke, Hants RG21 2BH. Tel: (01256) 469777.

Automobile Association & Touring Club of Greece (ELPA), Athens Tower, 2-4 Messogion Avenue, 1527 Athens. Tel: (01) 779 1615.

Auto Hellas S.A. (Hertz), 576 Vouliagmenis Avenue, 16451 Argyroupolis, Athens. Tel: (01) 994 2850 (renting and leasing of private cars).

Auto Route Europe; Next Base Limited, Headline House, Chanuer Road, Ashford, Middlesex TW15 2QT. Tel: (01784) 421422.

Avis, 48 Queen Amalia Avenue, Athens. Tel: (01) 322 4951.

Hellas Cars, 148 Syngrou Avenue, 17671 Athens. Tel: (01) 923 5353.

Motor Insurers Bureau, International Insurance Office, 4th Floor, 10 Xenofondos Street, 10557 Athens. Tel: (01) 323 6562.

RAC Travel Services, PO Box 499, South Croydon, Surrey CR2 62H. Tel: (0800) 550055.

PROPERTY ORGANISATIONS

Babet, The Mill House, Moorlands Road, Merriot, Somerset TA16 5NF. Tel: (01460) 76213. Properties for sale on the Peloponnese and Crete.

A P Bushell & Co, Peckwater House, Eddystone Road, Thurlestone, Kingsbridge, South Devon TQ7 3NU. Tel: (01548) 560370. Properties for sale.

John Chudleigh Properties. Tel: (0752) 22329. Specialising in land and property projects in Náfplion.

DTZ Mihalos, International Property Advisers, 7 Kriezotou Street, 10671 Athens. Tel: (01) 361 3101.

Fairways Club (Greece) Limited, 70 Agiou Alexandrou Street, 17561

P. Faliro, Athens. Tel: (01) 985 0166. Timeshare.

FOPDAC, Federation of Overseas Property Developers, Agents & Consultants, PO Box 3534, London NW5 1DQ. Tel: (020) 8744 2362.

John Goodwin Property Consultant, The Grange, Twiggs Lane, Marchwood, Southampton SO4 4UN. Tel: (01703) 864660. Properties for sale on the Peloponnese, Crete and Sporades Islands.

Home Finders International, 9 Thasou Street, Kastri, 14671 Athens. Tel: (01) 807 4570.

Knapp, Elise, Real Estate, Panepistmiou 6, 10671 Athens. Tel: (01) 364 3112.

Lambert Smith Hampton, Real Estate Consultants, 4 Sekeri Street, 10674 Athens. Tel: (01) 360 3667. Professional property advice.

Mavrelis Real Estate Agency, 180 Kifissias Avenue, 15231 Halandri, Athens. Tel: (01) 687 6360.

Property Owners Club, Britanny Ferries, Plymouth. Tel: (01752) 227941.

Susan Shimmin, 47 Kimpton House, Fontley Way, London SW15 4ND. Tel: (020) 8789 6372. Properties for restoration on the Peloponnese.

Sporades Properties, Walnut Cottage, Laverton, Nr Broadway, Worcestershire WR12 7NA. Tel: (01386) 73673. Properties for sale on the Sporades islands.

Timeshare Council, 23 Buckingham Gate, London SW1E 6LB. Tel: (020) 7821 8845.

Villa Owners Club Ltd, HPB House, Old Station Road, Newmarket CB8 8EH. Tel: (01638) 660066.

Whiteways Overseas Property Agents, 12 High Street, Knaresborough, North Yorkshire HG5 0EQ. Tel: (01423) 865892.

PUBLICATIONS

Army Geographical Service, Evelpídon 4, Nr Pedion Areos, Athens.

Athens News, 3 Christou Lada, 10237 Athens. Tel: (01) 322 4253.

Audience Research and Correspondence Department, Six Monthly Guide, BBC World Service, PO Box 76, Bush House, Strand, London WC2B 4PH. Tel: (020) 7257 8258.

BBC World Service, PO Box 3001, Central Post Office, Athens.

Greek-O-File, 4 Harvey Road, Langley, Berks SL3 8JB. Tel: (01753) 544475.

Hellenic Distribution Agency Limited, 1 Digeni Street, 17456 Alimos, Athens. Tel: (01) 991 9328 (national book distributors).

Hellenic Star, 10 Diocharous Street, Hilton Area, 11528 Athens. Greece's English Language and International Weekly.

International Herald Tribune, 57 Sokratous Street, 10431 Athens. Tel: (01) 529 9080.

Korfes Magazine (Mountaineering), Keutriki Platia, Aharnes, Athens. Tel: (01) 246 1528.

NSSG Likoúrgou 14, Omonia Square, Athens.

RELIGIOUS SERVICES

Anglican Chaplaincy

Anglican Evangelical Church, 12 PP Germenou Street, Thessaloniki. Tel: (031) 244 557.

San Francisco Church, Rhodes Town, Rhodes. Tel: 0241 23605.

Santa Maria Church, Niohuri, Rhodes. Tel: 0241 22305.

St Pauls Church, 27 Fillinon, Athens. Tel: (01) 323 4790.

St Peters Church (at St Catherine's British Embassy School), Sophocles Venizelou 73, Lykovrissi, Athens. Tel: (01) 807 5335.

Non denominational

St Andrews International Church, 66 Sina Street, Athens. Tel: (01) 645 2583.

Roman Catholic

Holy Apostles Church, 77 Alkyonidos & 1 Dafnis, Voula, Athens. Tel: (01) 985 8694.

Roman Catholic Church of St Pauls, 4 Kokkinaki, Kifissia, Athens. Tel: (01) 801 2526.

St Denis Roman Catholic Cathedral, 24 Panepistimiou, Athens. Tel: (01) 362 3603.

St John the Baptist Catholic Church, Papanastasiou Street, Paleo Psychico, Athens. Tel: (01) 671 1410.

St Pauls Roman Catholic Church, 4 Kokkinaki Street, Kifissia, Athens. Tel: (01) 801 2526.

Church of England

All Saints Church, Alkyonidos and Dafnis, Voula, Athens. Tel: (01) 895 8694.

Baptist

Grace Baptist Church, 4 Pringiponisson, Nea Ionia, Athens. Tel: (01) 964 9580.

Holy Trinity Church, 21M Mavilli Street, Corfu. Tel: 0661 31467.
Trinity Baptist Church, 58 Vouliagmenis, Ano Hellinikou, Athens. Tel:
(01) 962 1798.

Pentecostal

Hellenic Pentecostal Church (International Christian Fellowship),
Scripture Union Headquarters, 18 Tsaldari Street, Kifissia, Athens.
Tel: (01) 854 0513.
United Pentecostal Church International, 4-6 Poulion Ambelokipi,
Athens. Tel: (01) 645 3304.

REMOVAL FIRMS

Baxevanidis, 97 Syngrou Avenue, 11741 Athens. Tel: (01) 933 2146.
British Association of Removers, 3 Churchill Court, 58 Station Road,
North Harrow, Middlesex HA2 7SA. Tel: (020) 8861 3331.
Orpee Beinoglou, International Forwarders SA, Syngrou Avenue & 2A
Evripidou Street, Kallithea, 17674 Athens. Tel: (01) 942 1962.

SPORTS & RECREATION ORGANISATIONS

Amateur Anglers & Maritime Sports Club, Atkí Moutsópoulos, Piraeus.
Tel: (01) 411 5731.
Anglo Greek Club, Middlesex. Tel: (01895) 631865.
Anglo Greek Club, Worcester. Tel: (01905) 798453.
Association of Greek Camping, 102 Solonos Street, 10680 Athens. Tel:
(01) 362 1560.
Athens 2004 Olympics Organisational Committee, Zappion Megaro,
Athens.
Athens Riding Club. Tel: (01) 661 1088.
Athletic Riding Club of Ekali, Iraklio 6, Anoixi, Ekali, Nr Athens. Tel:
(01) 813 5576.
Federation of Excursion Clubs of Greece, 4 Drafatsaniou Street, Athens.
Tel: (01) 323 4107.
Glyfada Golf Club. Tel: (01) 894 6820.
Greek Cycling Federation, 28 Bouboulinas Street, Athens. Tel: (01) 883
1414.
Greek Sailing Club Federation, ISA Xenofóntos Street, Athens. Tel:
(01) 930 4826.
Greek Skiing and Alpine Federation, 7 Karageorgis Servia Street,
Athens. Tel: (01) 323 4555.

Greek Touring Club, 12 Politehniou Street, Athens. Tel: (01) 524 0854.

Greek Windsurfing Federation. Tel: (01) 413 7351.

Hellenic Federation of Mountaineering Clubs, 5 Milioni Street, Athens.

Hellenic Offshore Racing Club, 4 Popadiamanti Street, Mikros Limin, Piraeus. Tel: (01) 412 3357.

Hellenic Professional Yacht Owners Association, A8-A9 ZEA Marina, 18536 Piraeus. Tel: (01) 452 6335.

Hellenic Riding Club, Paradissou 18, Maroussi, Athens. Tel: (01) 682 6128.

Hellenic Rowing Federation, 34 Voukourestiou Street, Athens. Tel: (01) 361 2109.

Helmos Ski Centre, Peloponnese. Tel: (0692) 22174.

Hellenic Speleological Society, 8 Mantzarou Street, 10672 Athens. Tel: (01) 361 7824.

Hellenic Yachting Federation, Atki Navarchou, Kountouridti 7, 18534 Piraeus. Tel: (01) 413 7351.

Menalo Ski Centre, Peloponnese. Tel: (0712) 32243.

Pan Athenian Union of Baby Sitters, Glafkonos 5, Omonia Square, Athens. Tel: (01) 361 1685.

Piraeus Yacht Club, 18 Kar Servias Street, 18535 Piraeus, Nr Athens. Tel: (01) 413 3489.

Tennis Federation of Greece, Vasilissis Olgas 2, Athens. Tel: (01) 921 5630.

Trehantiri, 365–367 Green Lanes, Haringey, London N4 1DY. Tel: (020) 8802 6530. (Largest Greek music selection in the world.)

Union of Greek Diving Centre. Tel: (01) 922 9532.

Water Skiing Association, 32 Stournara Street, Athens. Tel: (01) 523 1875.

TAXATION AUTHORITIES

Inland Revenue International Division (Double Taxation), Strand Bridge House, 138–142 The Strand, London WC2R 1HH.

Inland Revenue, Overseas Advice Dept, Public Enquiry Room, West Wing, Somerset House, London WC2R 1LB. Tel: (020) 7438 6622.

Inland Revenue, Pensions and Dividends Overseas Dept, Lynwood Road, Thames Ditton, Surrey KT7 0DP. Tel: (020) 8398 4242.

Ministry of Finance, Ypourgio Ikonomikon, Tmima Diethon Scheseon, Sina Street 2-4, 10184 Athens. Tel: (01) 360 4825.

TRAVEL AND TOURISM ORGANISATIONS

Agoudimos Lines, 46 Ethnikis Antistasis Street, Igoumenitsa, Greece. Tel: (0665) 23630 (Adriatic sea crossings).

American Express International SA, 2 Ermou Street, PO Box 3325, 10225 Athens. Tel: (01) 322 0486.

Apollonian Travel, 3 Holwood Cottages, Saltash, Cornwall PL12 5AL. Tel: (01752) 851681.

Argo Travel. Tel: (020) 7935 2006. Source of inexpensive scheduled flights.

Athens International Airport, 5thkm Spata-Loutsa Avenue, Spata, 19004 Attiki. Tel: (01) 369 8300.

Athens & Piraeus Electric Railway Company (ISAP), 67 Athinas Street, 10552 Athens. Tel: (01) 324 8311.

Attiko Metro, 191–193 Messogion Avenue, 11525 Athens. Tel: (01) 679 2399.

British Airways PLC, Vouliagmenis 130 & Thmistokleous 1, Glyfada, 16674 Athens. Tel: (01) 890 6611.

British Midland, 65b Vouliagmenis & 29 Achilleous, Glyfada, 16674 Athens. Tel: (01) 960 0943.

British Rail European Travel Centre, Victoria Station, London SW1. Tel: (020) 7834 9656.

Co-Op Travel Club, PO Box 53, 1st Floor, Corporation Street, Manchester M60 4ES. Tel: (0161) 832 4353 (major travel club offering substantial discounts on flights and travel insurance).

Cronus Airlines, 517 Vouliagmenis Avenue & Agiou Ioannoul, Elioupoli, 16341 Athens. Tel: (01) 995 6400.

Easyjet Airline Co Ltd, Easyland, London Luton Airport, Luton LU2 9LS. Tel: (0777) 575 1651.

Eurolines (UK) Ltd, (National Express Group Company), 4 Cardiff Road, Luton.

Greek Civil Aviation Authority, 1 Vas. Georgiou Street, Helliniko, Athens. Tel: (01) 894 4263.

Greek Railways Organisation (OSE), 1–3 Karolou Street, 10437 Athens. Tel: (01) 524 2205.

Greek State Tourist Office (EOT), 4 Conduit Street, London W1R D02. Tel: (020) 7734 5997.

Karageorgis Lines, 36 King Street, London WC2E 8JS. Tel: (020) 7836 821.

Manos (UK) Ltd, 168-172 Old Street, London EC1V 9BP. Tel: (020) 7216 8040 (flight consolidator).

Manos Travel System SA, 6-10 Charilaou Trikoupi, 10679 Athens. Tel: (01) 360 2734 (flight consolidator).

Mediterranean Passenger Services, 9 Hanover Street, London W1R 8HF. Tel: (020) 7499 0076.

National Tourist Organisation, 2 Amerikis Street,   10564 Athens. Tel: (01) 322 3111.

National Tourist Organisation of Greece (NTOG), 4 Conduit Street, London W1R 0DJ. Tel: (020) 7734 5997.

Olympic Airways, 6 Othonos Street, Syntagma Square, Athens. Tel: (01) 929 2555.

Peloponnese Walking Tour Company. Tel: (01905) 798453 (UK), (0721) 73919 (Greece). Web: www.zyworld.com/stafeeli/walk tours.htm

Pioneer Tours, 11 Nikis Street, Syntagma Square, 10557 Athens. Tel: (01) 322 4321.

P & O European Ferries, Channel House, Channel View Road, Dover, Kent CT17 9TJ. Tel: (01304) 203388.

Royal Olympic Cruises, 87 Akti Miaouli, Piraeus 18538. Tel: 429 1000.

Swiss National Tourist Office, Swiss Court, London W1V 8EE. Tel: (020) 7734 1921.

Thessalonikí Metro, 45 Eleftheriou Venizelou Street, 54631 Thessalonikí. Tel: (031) 238 321.

Trading Places. Tel: (020) 7962 9028. Source of inexpensive charter flights.

Transalpino, 71-75 Buckingham Palace Road, London SW1. Tel: (020) 7834 9656.

Trekking 7 Filelinon Street, 10557 Athens. Tel: (01) 331 0323.

Usit/Eurotrain, 52 Grosvenor Gardens, London SW1W 0AG. Tel: (020) 7730 3402.

Virgin Atlantic Airlines Limited, Ashdown House, High Street, Crawley, West Sussex RH10 1DQ. Tel: (01293) 562345.

Virgin Atlantic Airways Ltd, 70 Panormou Street, 11523 Athens. Tel: (01) 690 5300.

Viamare Travel Limited, Graphic House, 2 Sumatra Road, London NW6 1PU. Tel: (020) 7431 4560.

Wexas International Travel Club, 45-49 Brompton Road, London WS3 1DE. Tel: (020) 7589 0500 (major travel club offering substantial discounts on flights and travel insurance).

UTILITIES

Athens Water and Sewage Company (EYDAP), 156 Oropou Street, Galatsi, 11146 Athens. Tel: (01) 253 3402.

OTEnet AE, 56 Kifissias Avenue, Maroussi, 15125 Athens. Tel: (01) 619 8320.

Public Gas Corporation of Greece (DEPA) SA, 207 Messogion Avenue, 11525 Athens. Tel: (01) 647 9106–9.

Public Power Corporation of Greece (PPS) SA, 30 Halkokondili Street, 10432 Athens. Tel: (01) 523 0301.

YOUTH HOSTELS

87 Alexandras Avenue, 11474 Athens. Tel: (01) 646 3669.

75 Damareous Street, Pangrati, Athens. Tel: (01) 751 9530.

Greek Youth Hostels HQ, Dragatsaniou 4, 7th Floor, Platía Klafthmónos, Athens.

3 Hamilton & 97B Patission, 10434 Athens. Tel: (01) 822 0328.

16 Victor Hugo Street, Nr Vathis Square, Athens. Tel: (01) 523 4170.

20 Kalipoleos Street, Vyronas, 16232 Athens. Tel: (01) 766 4889.

57 Kypselis Street, 11361 Athens. Tel: (01) 822 5860.

YMCA (XAN) Acadimias & Omirou Street, Athens. Tel: (01) 363 6970.

YWCA (XEN), 11 Amerikis Street, 10672 Athens. Tel: (01) 362 4291.

Glossary

Throughout this book I have aimed to be as consistent as possible with the phonetic spelling of Greek words, *eg* K instead of C, O instead of A. Also to help the reader I have put accents on words to indicate the pronunciation stress points. Unfortunately, space has not permitted use of the ancient Greek letters, but to help you on your way, I set out below the 24 letter alphabet:

A	α	alfa	N	ν	nee
B	β	veeta	Ξ	ξ	ksee
Γ	γ	ghama	O	o	omeekron
Δ	δ	dhelta	Π	π	pee
E	ε	ep-seelon	P	ρ	ro
Z	ζ	zeeta	Σ	σ	seeghma
H	η	eeta	T	τ	taf
Θ	θ	theeta	Y	υ	eepseelon
I	ι	yota	Φ	φ	fee
K	κ	kapa	X	χ	khee
Λ	λ	landha	Ψ	ψ	spee
M	μ	mee	Ω	ω	omegha

Ad hoc. For a particular purpose only.
Ad infinitum. Endlessly.
Andhrón. Gentlemen's toilets.
Ad nauseam. To a great extent.
Avrio. Tomorrow, which perhaps never comes.
Baklávas. Wonderful honey and nut pastry creation.
Bona fide. Undertaken in good faith.
Bros. The welcoming 'who's there' Greek method of answering the telephone.

Caveat emptor. Let the buyer beware — he bears the risk.

Chryssos odigos. Greek telephone directory, a little like our *Yellow Pages*.

Dhomatia. Rooms to let.

Dimarchio. Town Hall.

Dimmossia Steria Ilektrismou. National electricity company (DEH).

ELPA. Greek equivalent of AA/RAC.

Enikiassis akinitou. Property to rent section in local newspaper.

Enikiazete. 'To let' signs found on walls and doors.

Estiatório. Restaurant or taverna.

Esoterikó. Post box for local mail.

Exoterikó. Post box for overseas mail.

Fakellos. Envelopes.

Farmakío. Pharmacy.

Filoxenía. The wonderful warm Greek friendship.

Frondistíria. English language school in Greece.

Galaktobóureko. Creamy custard pie.

Grafia Evrésseos Ergassiás. Greek private employment agency.

Grammatósima. Postage stamps.

Gynaikon. Ladies' toilets.

Hérete. Welcome, alternate to *Yá sas*.

Horiátiki. World famous Greek salad.

Iatrico Vivliario. Medical booklet you need to take on all visits to doctor or hospital.

Idrima Kinonikon Asfalisseon. Greek national health system (IKA).

Iperastikó. Long distance calls.

Ipiresía Allodhapóu. The aliens department, where queuing becomes an art form.

Ippódromos. Horse race track.

Kafenío. Coffee shop and centre of local gossip.

Kafés frappé. Ice cold coffee in a long glass.

Kaikía. Small island hopping boats.

Kaló Taxídhi. We wish you well on your journey.

Kataífi. Delicious shredded wheat covered in honey.

Katapígonda. Post Office 'express' services should reduce delivery time to UK by 2-3 days.

KKE. Minority communist party in Greece.

Kombolói. Infamous Greek worry beads.

Krasí dopio. House wine.

Kréma. Smooth, custardy semolina often served with cinnamon.

KTEL. Private consortium of Greek coaches.

Linenarhió. Local port police.

Loghareeasmó. Restaurant receipt.

Mezédhes. *Hors d'oeuvres*; collection of pieces of fish, meat, cheese, olives, bread *etc* served on cocktail sticks, normally as an accompaniment to *Oúzo*.

Nea Demokrati. Conservative party in Greece.

Nefos. Fog, or pollution cloud found in Athens.

Organisimos Apasholisseos Ergatiko Dynamikou. Greek family and unemployment agency (OAED).

Organismos Telepikinonion Ellados. National telecommunications company (OTE).

Oúzo. Aniseed based apéritif.

Pagotó. Ice cream.

Pagotó me Méli. Ice cream with honey — you could be in heaven.

Panagiriá. A party usually celebrating a name-sake day.

PASOK. Labour Party in Greece.

Períptero. Street kiosk loaded with everything you can imagine.

Poste Restante. Facility for Post Office to hold mail on your behalf.

Prima facie. First Class, evidence of a fact.

Pro rata. In proportion.

Psarotavérnes. Taverna specialising in fish.

Psistariés. Taverna specialising in spit roasted meats.

Quid pro quo. Given in exchange for something else.

Rizógalo. Smooth, creamy rice pudding often served with cinnamon.

Sistiméno. Registered delivery.

Skorpédia, Weekly refuse collection.

Souvláki. Pork kebabs on short wooden sticks.

Status quo. The existing state of affairs.

Stremmatta. A quarter of an acre to build on, maybe!

Tachidromío. Post office.

Távli. Backgammon.

Telonía. Customs authority.

Topikó. Local calls.

Toualéta. Toilets.

Touristiki astinomiá. Tourist police.

Touristiki grafió. Local tourism office. Good source of accommodation.

Trápeza. Bank.

Vignette. Tax disk needed to drive on Swiss motorways.

Volta. The evening parade looking your finest.

Ya sás. Hello, also used as goodbye.

Yátria. Out patients' clinic.

Yenikó Nosokomío. Lowest grade of state hospital.

Yiaoúrti. Greek yoghurt, particularly lovely when mixed with garlic, lemon and cucumber to make *Tzatzíki*.

Zaharoplastía. After dinner meeting places for sticky pastries and coffee.

Index